Dîvân-i Kebîr

Meter II
Bahr-i Muzari
-Ariz-

Mevlâna Celâleddîn Rumi

Ministry of Culture Publications of the Republic of Turkey / 1761

Dîvân-i Kebîr

Meter II
Bahr-i Muzari
-Ariz-

Mevlâna Celâleddîn Rumi

Translated by Nevit Oguz Ergin

Echo Publications
Sun Valley, California, United States

Dîvân-i Kebîr

Copyright © 1995 by
Nevit Oguz Ergin
&
Turkish Republic Ministry of Culture

All rights are reserved. Reproductions in any manner, in whole or in part, in English or in other languages, or otherwise, without written permission of the publisher is prohibited.

ISBN 1-887991-00-X

First Printing 1995
Printed in the United States of America
in a joint publication by

Turkish Republic
Ministry of Culture

&

Echo Publications
8258 Sunland Boulevard
Sun Valley, California 91352

Introduction

At the suggestion of the government of Turkey, 1995 was announced by the United Nations as the Year of Tolerance throughout the world.

The notion of tolerance has spread throughout the year as the most needed, but at the same time the most ignored, concept of the twentieth century. During that year we have tried to explain the meaning of tolerance from Anatolia, the home of some of the most important names of those who have championed tolerance throughout the whole world.

I have no doubt that this invitation to the tolerance of humanity, which Turkey started in 1995, will find its place in everybody's heart and cause their sincere contribution to that call.

When we mention tolerance, one of the first names that come to mind is Mevlâna Celâleddîn. Abdulbaki Gölpinarli's seven volumes of contemporary Turkish translation of the Divan, which is based on Mevlaâna Celâleddins's two volumes of the most reliable Dîvân-i Kebîr (registered at the library of Konya Mevlana Museum) was published in 1992 by our Ministry.

The Dîvân-i Kebîr is co-published, this time in English, with the participation of our Ministry and a publisher in the United States. This is the completed second volume of the Dîvân. The first volume has already been published.

I leave all of humanity alone with the words of Mevlâna, and I wish happy days in a world full of peace and more tolerance.

D. Fikri Saglar
Minister of Culture
Republic of Turkey

Leather binding (c. 1368) of *Divân-i Kebîr* registered at the Mevlana Museum in Konya.

Müstef ilün faulün Müstef ilün faulün

First page, Gazel 1, Verse 1 of Bahr-i Muzari-Ariz- of the Dîvân-i Kebîr (c.1368) registered at the Mevlana Museum in Konya, Turkey. Müstef ilün faulün Müstef ilün faulün represents the rhyme scheme of the meter.

Translator's Note

This is a humble attempt at an English translation of the late distinguished Turkish Scholar Abdülbâki Gölpinarli's (d. 1982) seven volumes of the *Dîvân-i Kebîr* of Mevlânâ Celâleddin.

According to Gölpinarli, his translation of the *Dîvân* was based on the following sources:

1. Two volumes of the *Dîvân*, which were compiled between July 2, 1367 and October 12, 1368 by Hasan ibni Osman-al Mavlavi. This *Dîvân* has 290 pages, and the volume dimensions are 0.325x0.47 meters. It is registered at the Mevlânâ Museum in Konya as No. 68 and No. 69.

2. The *Dîvân* registered at the Library of the University of Istanbul, No. 334, which was compiled in the 15th century.

3. The *Dîvân* owned by Gölpinarli, prepared in 1691 in Baghdad. Later, this *Dîvân* was donated to the Mevlânâ Museum in Konya.

4. Eight volumes of *Kulliyat-i Shems ya Divan Kebîr* prepared by Bedî-uz-Zaman Furûzan-fer, in 1965 (1345 S.H.).

There are many other versions of the *Dîvân-i Kebîr*, but these are the most dependable ones

Mevlânâ did not write, but rather recited the poems. Most of them were recorded by assigned people called Secretaries of Secret (Katibal esrar).

The *Dîvân*'s language is 13th century colloquial Farsi. However, there are numerous *gazels*, or poems, written in Arabic and Greek. In addition, there are Turkish words and phrases spread throughout the *Dîvân*'s pages.

There are 21 meters in the *Dîvân*. The first volume has 12,493 verses; the second has 4,052; the third has 4,526; the fourth has 4,180; the fifth has 6,684; the sixth has 4,002; and the seventh has 8,892. All together, the *Dîvân* has 44,829 verses.

We started with the first meter, *Bahr-i Recez*. In the original *Dîvân-i Kebîr*, the meters were compiled according to their ending rhyme scheme and the last alphabet letter of their rhyme, not in chronological order. This second meter has the rhyme scheme *Mustefilun Faulun Mustefilun Faulun*.

I am grateful to the Ministry of Culture of Turkey for their continued support and encouragement.

I am also indebted to Mrs. Terry Peart for the years she has spent, not only reading my handwriting, but understanding, typing, and editing it.

I would especially like to thank my dear friend Mr. Veli Kalay of Turkey for all the support and encouragement he has given me.

It is with great excitement and humility that I bring this treasure, in its entirety for the first time, to the English-speaking world.

Nevit Oguz Ergin
Translator

1.

Verse 2093

For some time he has poured
So much wine on our soil
That there is a yell and scream
In every particle of our earth and body.

Our chest is split wide open.
Our hearts start weaving love
With the Almighty's cup.
Our glass is cleaned and purified.

Though flowers have bloomed,
Bad eyes don't see them.
Zeal says to me, "Don't drool, drink the wine."

O Soul, as soon as you appeared
You snatched my heart and soul.
Because you were the customer,
The garment became valuable.

Your cloud rains grass.
Your glass gives soul.
Your trouble sets inside so nicely,
Don't add anymore.

O love, I will be drunk with your wine
As long as I am alive.
When I approach the
"He-drew-near-then-nearer" level.[1]
I am exalted with your kindness,
I am down with your kindness.

How can I call you moon?
The moon has fever and becomes pale.
It is true I could call you cypress,
But the cypress can be burned.

The moon hasn't shown the last three nights.
There is no substance to anything
But the source of the source of the soul.

The moon and sun eclipse.
If you are the Abraham of the time,
Tell them you don't want them.
Turn your face away from them.

They say, "All our friends have died, are gone."
The one who loves God
Lives with His love and never dies.

The fountain of life is God.
The soul will be slave to
The one who escapes to God.
Gabriel will be his nanny.

Beside the laughter which comes from Soul
With the Grace of God,
The laughter of these people
Is like lightning,
It comes and goes.

2.

Verse 2105

O, watermaster, open the fountain.
Let the garden be awakened,
The eyes of the flower be opened.

In the darkness of your eyes
Your kindness is hidden
Like the fountain of life.
With those pupils, he turns the eyes
Into a sea.

Without your favor,
Neither the people, nor the embryo
Inside the womb would move.

Moving in the womb or in absence is nothing.
Even the bones in the grave
Dance with your radiance.

We dance around a lot
With the tunes of this world.
Come on friends, be ready
For the dance in another world.

Souls are moving with these rough, coarse covers.
Once they throw these heavy covers off,
Watch their dances.

Before birth, we were kicking
And moving in the darkness
Of the womb
Just to express our sincere thanks.

We are all Sufis
Who came dancing from the dervish convent
To give thanks for these free blessings.

It is proper to give our life
For these blessings.
What is life for
But this generous treasure?

The sky is the top of this cup,
Which contains earth's blessings.
How can I talk about the dining table?

We are Sufis on the journey.
Eat the blessings of our Sultan.
May God make this cup,
This table, eternal.[2]

We have nothing but an empty cup
To hold the Sultan's favors.
We have no profit
But to extend our cup
For those blessings.
In any case, the wrong one
Could not get this bowl, this bread.

To the fly—the creature which
Gives shame to the host—
There is no difference between
A bowl full of blessings
And an empty, dirty one.

But the true one sometimes
Bites his tongue,
Even without seeing and tasting,
And keeps his silence.
At other times, he starts talking
And praising them.

3.

Verse 2119

I expelled all the philosophical denials
From my heart entirely.
I purified my heart.
I put the forms that belonged to Joseph
In my eye.

It should be a beauty unseen
And impossible for worlds to praise.
Like Adam in front
Falls down and worships.

This is an imperial cipher.
With a kind of radiance of its own.
Every moment gives a glow.
Every extinguished light.
Burn them, light them.

When the sun rises,
Every particle appears.
It would be necessary that a secret particle
Would need another light to shine.

The source of existence is that
Sea of abundance which has
Been catching all unseemly things.

4.

Verse 2124
Tercî-Bend

O sparing cupbearers,
Love is increased
And increased again.
Give color to these pale faces.

O, Master of cupbearers,
O, One who holds
The hand of my soul,
O, my Master,
This is the time for business.
Act bravely.

Beloved, the mind is your drunk,
So is the soul.
What are you holding in your hand?
Bring it forth, put it in front.
Don't hide it.

O, One who makes the sky restless,
The mind drunk,
Open your arms just once.
I fell in depression, depression.

O, greatest of Futu-i vet[3]
O, introduction of the Books of the Prophet,
O, Sultan of humanity,
Don't eat halva alone.

You have escaped from us
And gone far away,
Holding a mirror to hide
Your face from others.

O, One whose face
Is like the sun,
They open a window at every stop,
Every staging place,
So the Universe will be illuminated by You.

If you don't drink this,
And have no mercy for me,
I'll write a new Terci.
Maybe you'll be enthusiastic with that one.

———

O, light of the eyes of Soul,
You'll guide us like eyes.
The Soul tried that, O Beloved.
You are adding soul to his Soul.

Wherever Soul turns its face,
It turns to You,
But still doesn't know
Where You are, O Soul.

Wherever You are, You call
Elest's invitation.[4]
You make us drunk,
Give us existence
With Your generosity and kindness.

You give temptation to the heart.
Pull in every direction.
Sometimes You lead us to the bottom,
At other times, drag us to joy and happiness.

If you want to help, gain something.
Hopelessness will cease immediately.
Even the dog that took refuge in your cave
Became a saint.[5]

When a man runs that direction,
The moon rises from Your sky
And reflects on him, lighting his way.
He acquires the property of Absence
And the mind of consent.

Who can tell anything about Him?
When the needy look for Him,
He fills their pockets with gold.
When the poor look for Him,
Just to be kind, He acts like a beggar.
He becomes the beggar's beggar.

Now, tell all its branches and roots
In different ways.
Show this hidden sea.
Bring its track to the surface.

―――

When I start to talk
About the Beloved,
I lose my heart.
Once I lose myself,
How can I look for Him?

It is all His decision.
What do I say?
For what do I search?
He is the cupbearer.
He is the final One.
I am only a ladle.

If I am a thorn, a porcupine,
You turn me into silk.
I have a thousand layers.
I became a string on this road.

If I kiss you once,
I will become the Holy Ghost, like Jesus.
If I smell your apple,
I will give my soul, like Moses.

I am an old ruined house,
Saved for your treasure.
You are the fountain of life.
I lay under your feet, like a river.

I used to hang around people.
I was magnanimous and tolerant of everyone.
I am changed
In order not to have anybody else.
My heart has become very narrow now.

Because of your peerless beauty
And very delicate image,
My love, even my worries,
Have lost their confidentiality.
Nobody understands anything from me.

Love came as a rushing torrent
From the great abyss.
For God's sake,
Build a dam for this torrent.

5.

Verse 2148

Somebody is hidden.
Don't think yourself alone.
Someone hears with sharp ears.
Don't say bad things.

That fairy put an obstacle
At the springs of the Heart.
Every form that comes to your
Imagination is from that fairy.

One has to be very cautious
When going near the fountains,
Because there are lots of fairies there.

As long as the springs of these five senses
Keep running in your body,
That fairy opens the dikes
And lets those five springs flow away.

Let those springs flow away
Through your five inner senses,
Like imagaination, surmise, and other perceptions.

Every spring has two fortresses
And fifty passengers.
If you clean the mirror of your heart
They show their faces to you.

If you don't follow good manners
At the source of the water,
You suffer from fairies
Because this kind of fairy is hard and ferocious.

It doesn't matter how hard you work,
Fate always spoils the measures.
His rules carry away
The carpets of hundreds like us.

Look at those birds in the cage,
Those fish in the net.
Watch all the hearts crying
Because of this deceitful beauty.

Don't look at every beauty
With evil eyes,
So that beautiful Sultan
Won't give you up.

There are a few verses left,
But that spring is dried.
Maybe tomorrow we will jump,
And that spring will start flowing again.

6.

Verse 2159

The spring of Souls has come.
Dance, O green branches.
Sugar came to this world
Like Joseph returned to Egypt.
Start dancing.

O Sultan who grows with love
Like a baby with its mother's milk,
Come, be exuberant.
O Soul of his father, get in the dance.

You came running like a ball
After seeing His hair,
Which resembles the club.
You gave up your head, your feet,
And danced without head or feet.

A bloody murderer came suddenly,
With the sword in his hand,
And asked me how I am.
I said, "Good news, I hope."
"No," he answered, "It is evil,
Start dancing."

With love, even kings turn
Into rain in His sky.
What's the use of a caftan?
O, one who has this beautiful belt,
Start dancing.

Oh, you who are drunk with your own being,
Absence is written on you.
The decree of Absence came to you.
Be ready for the journey.
Start dancing.

My beauty came walking
With the wine cup in his hand.
If you are not a woman, start dancing
With the love of this male lion.

The war is ended.
The harp is playing.
Joseph got out of the well.
O clumsy, no-good one,
Start dancing.

How long will these promises last?
How long will this head stay in prostration?
How long will I stay on the floor in worship?
How long is this separation which will ruin colors
And works in which I am involved?
Come, start dancing.

When will he tell me, that one
Who is not aware of anything, to get lost?
The one who is aware of everything,
Get up, start dancing.

When will our peacock come,
Those colors appear,
And tell the Bird of Soul,
"Come and dance without wings, without arms?"

The deaf and blind
Have found their cures from Jesus.
Mary's son, Jesus, told them,
"O deaf and blind, keep dancing."

Shems is the one who became an idol, a deity.
Even China is jealous of Tebriz.
Oh branches, trees, dance.
Dance in the spring of his beauty.

7.

Verse 2172

You brought the wine of eternity,
But we couldn't enjoy drinking
Even one cup of this wine.

Play, leave the glass.
Play this kind of wail.
O Soul, try to price that priceless beauty.

Price the chain of love that ties you.
That calamity, the well of Babil,
That mine of spells.

Bring it back.
Offer that cup again,
That our affairs will turn into pure gold
To return to the customs of loyalty.

Even the devil,
Whose essence is kneaded by evil,
Becomes an angel with your favor.
Your imperial cipher is drawn
To the country of cleanliness and truth.

Oh, chosen man. Oh, exalted one.
I see Mohammed's glory every moment
In your radiance.

Once roads are folded,
Everything in my hand turns into a sigh.
Even mountains become a piece of straw
Against Love that resembles amber.

Only Tebriz understands Shems.
Who, like a moon
Hears the praying, but says Amen
Every once in a while.

8.

Verse 2180

Arouse the music and joy.
Give yourself to me, follow me.
Turn your face from evil eyes.
Look at me.

To be enlivened,
Give yourself to me,
Then read that dependable spell.
Breathe on death, like Jesus.

Oh, One whose face
Is more beautiful than the moon,
Put Your face over mine
So your slave would
See eternal prosperity.

Once you said,
"This kiss is only
For the engaged ones."
I saw in my dream, it was me.
I was kissing your sweet lips,
Tasting that sugar.

O, my God,
What would happen to the angels
If the verse of
"Nobody could be His son,"[6]
Appeared on His face?
If He made His matchlessness
Known to the universe?

Since I have held your hand
I haven't seen anyone.
But I have gone so far from myself
That no reason, no mind, is left.
Everything there has disappeared.

Offer that pomegranate-colored cup.
Fill it up to the rim
So my eyes will be full.
No envy will be left.

Offer the wine that comes
From the height of the assembly of
"There is no One but Him to be worshipped."[7]
There, Soul sees God
And breaks and destroys the mold.

Once the mirror of the mind
Is out of its woolen cover,
You can beat the wool
As much as you want.

9.

Verse 2189

O, watermaster of the water of Soul,
Break the jar, break the carafe
So eyes will be open
Like bowls in front of You.

Strike our nonsense.
O, One who blows our minds,
Make man confused.
Strike, so that this mind will give up
All these trials, all this silliness.

Since You broke the bell of body,
Take the modesty from the mind
So that sneak can do no harm.

If he casts a spell and ties people's tongues,
You walk like Moses' staff
And untie tongues.

Lovers should be silenced.
It is better for the sea to boil up.
But the words have been spoken in silence
Resembling images on the face of a mirror.
They look better.

10.

Verse 2194

*B*eloved, be tolerant to our searching.
We are the creatures of love,
The disciples of love.
Grab our hair and pull us toward You.

The rose is prostrate in front of us
After seeing our faces
When You have offered us
Tulip-colored wine
Without a glass or jar.

Make our eyes drunk, sleepy,
And tender today.
Change our village so much that
Even Heaven will be jealous of it.

We resemble the gold and silver mine.
No one is an enemy of gold.
We are the ones who give prosperity
To our friends, as well as our enemies.

We turn into the candles of Taraz.[8]
We get taller, our heads get higher,
Our necks grow, our hearts get spacious.
You made all these things with that wine.

O, Fountain of Life,
Your torrent snatches us,
Breaks our jar now.

If you don't know our disposition,
Ask it of the charm of wine.
It turned our disposition into wine.

Even if You pour the sea,
We can't be filled our satisfied.
Because You put the scoop
To our mouths upside down.

Another guest came.
Pick up another cup
Because this one doesn't
Have enough even to wash us.

Look, a bunch of drunks are
Coming to the garden.
How could they resist?
They get our smell.

If Mercury had heard our guiding voice,
It would have given up its talent
And erased all its notebooks.

The one who falls in love and boasts
Will be beaten like a tambourine.
You pick up the plectrum,
Play our three-stringed instrument.

It is enough. Be silent now.
If they hear the gossip of our words,
Suddenly, even Earth will become a bitter place
For the worldly.

11.

Verse 2207

Now, I've set a nice trap for that beauty
Who became Kible[9] to our eyes.
I'll catch that beauty who is
The essence of all forms and beauties.

There is an ear on the wall.
O, mind, go to the roof and watch.
O, heart, lock your door.

Enemies are waiting in ambush.
If they hear, they will talk to each other,
And make a lot of gossip.

From this heart
A world of secrets were heard.
He runs to the enemies
And tells them, one by one.
True or false, he told all of them.

Even particles are hidden.
They are enemies to each other.
They talk at the bottom of the well.
If you look for privacy,
Choose the early dawn.

O Soul, one day, not the enemy
But the image of the enemy,
While passing by,
Stopped in my heart.

Since then we decided,
The beloved and I,
To hide the secret.
Bend our head down.

We are also brave men.
We are not worse than
The stone cover of the mine.
The mine doesn't show its gold
Without being hit by the pick.

Even the sea tightened its purse,
Frowned, sour-faced, and said,
"Where did I see the pearl?
I don't know anything."

12.

Verse 2216

The ones who meet you
Add hundreds of souls to their soul.
But when you meet a woman
You become withered;
Your backbone loosened.

Because to meet the dead,
Freeze the body,
Look at all these early people.
Understand.

Their rulers are worn out.
So are the merchants.
Throw dirt to the heads
Of these kinds of beauties.

Go and see the beauties in divine love.
Their faces light up
And adorn the whole sky.

A secret Beauty offered youth
As a gift to every old man.
Look at the soul coming
To the Judas tree from that house.

If you don't stop talking,
I'll leave here.
Look at that sinister tongue of yours.
Close your mouth.

13.

Verse 2222

Untie your hair, which spreads ambergris.
Put the soul of Sufis to dancing.

The sun, moon, and stars
Are turning around the sky.
We are in the middle.
Turn the one in the middle.

Your singing and playing is such a favor,
Even the lowest tones in the melody
Start turning the Sufis of the sky.

The spring breeze comes running,
Singing and making the world smile.
It causes a commotion among the young.

How many sneaks become friends?
The rose and thorn are one of a pair.
Kindness of time turns the garden
Into the likeness of a Sultan

The garden turns within,
Gains distance and tells you,
"You. too, reach the end
Of the road from within.
To Soul would be added your soul."

At last, a bud opens,
Whispers the secrets of the iris and cypress.
The tulip gives good news, with the willow,
To the Judah tree.

Secrets of every sampling
Raise their heads from the bottom,
Then grow taller and spread.
The Ones resurrected
Put letters from the gardens to the sky.

Birds and nightingales
Are in the branches like guards.
They get their sustenance from treasure.

These leaves resemble tongues.
This fruit is like hearts.
When hearts smile,
The ties of the tongues will loosen.
Words will become valuable.

14.

Verse 2232

The stars remarked, "It is very bright tonight."
When I heard that, I said to the stars,
"For sure, the Moon is with me tonight."

Climb the roof of greatness
To call everybody; to talk with them.
Tonight is the night to gather roses.
Tonight is the night to drink wine.

Our beloved has been in our arms
Until morning, like a heart.
His hands have been around
Our neck tonight.

Negroes have been fighting with
The people of Rum until morning.[10]
Musicians have been singing
Their musical rhythm[11] from morning 'til night.

Wine glasses have been
Turning around until morning.
Favors are coming.
The rose and iris have been
In privacy, night until morning.

I will offer the wine of Union
To the people, prominent or not,
To everyone.
The Beauty with a moon face
Is at the window looking at us.
I will offer the wine with that joy, to everybody.

Iron has been softening and turning into wax
The same way it happened to David.
Because the Beloved is a magnet,
Heart is iron tonight.

Untie the hands of the heart
So he can put his head on the feet of Love.
Because that poor one who has been crying
And waiting because of evil eyes
Is in a safe place tonight.

O, fortune, keep kissing my
Golden, pale face, because
Cut, chipped gold has returned
And is mine again.

The one who constantly tries
To stage a hold-up, deceiving us,
Should have the saddle of the donkey on his back.
He is so confused, so stupid tonight.

His sharpened sword doesn't work.
It looks like it is wooden tonight.
His long spear turned into
A small needle tonight.

His inaccessible fortress
Looks like a spider's web.
His armor, his horse's bit
Melted like oil tonight.

Be silent! Because the one
Who desires and expects is always lisping.
Why are you betting with him?
He is lisping tonight.

15.

Verse 2245

O soul of hundreds, on Regaib's night[12]
Pay attention to lovers,
Sit among the drunks.
Here is the moon, here are the stars.

That day which hasn't been
Seen by anyone is full of wonders;
Turned out to be a day of resurrection,
Is submerged in wonders and
Has disappeared in the face of your beauty.

"Clean things," you said, "are for the clean."[13]
But who is more clean than you are,
O mine of cleanliness?

A kingdom is given to soul
Every moment from you.
Who should I thank for that?
The Sultan, or the doorkeeper?

You put clean-hearted ones under the ground.
They all bend their heads to their mantles
Like Sufis in meditation.

Once your love came,
Thoughts died in front of Him.
Your love is the real dawn,
Mind is a phoney morning.

O mind, don't look
For either Union or Separation.
How can you desire to meet
Someone who is not absent?

What is Soul? Absence? Need?
Who is the One who gives Soul?
Oh, the Kible of needs,
The sweetheart of demands.

Now the last day of judgment has come.
Here is the sign of it:
The sun rose from the west.

O One who pulls so great,
Pull the one who is scared,
The ones who are in trouble,
With one of your Soul's pullings.

Pull, that these two eyes
See the daybreak of God's morning,
The net of desire torn to pieces,
And understand
That the One who was desired
Is the One who desires.

What is Love's desire?
The mirror of manifestation.
What are Self and Greed?
The mirror of shame.

Where is the nightingale of the garden?
I will tell words to him
That have never been told
Nor written by anybody.

Those words are not for
The design of forms,
Nor pure things, nor turbid;
Not for past, nor present,
Not for asceticism, nor presence.

I have lost my mind.
You tell the rest
O One from whose door
Nobody has ever returned deprived,
Without reaching his hope.

16.

Verse 2260

The works of lovers
Turned into gold tonight.
The souls of the greedy
Are blind and deaf tonight.

God's beautiful sea became rough.
Waves overflowed.
The dirt on the road
Became amber with His arrival.

We are pleasant, good all the time,
But with the Grace of God,
We are different tonight.
He is different tonight.

Don't turn your face away.
He is such a friend, next to you.
Bend your head down, because this
Head is good and drunk from that.

Since He came to hold your hand,
Clap your hands and dance tonight.
A branch of the Kingdom
Is green and fresh tonight.

I swear to God,
Sleep is forbidden to me tonight,
Because the Soul, which looks like a water bird,
Plunged into the Kevser.[14]

17.

Verse 2266

Today our town is so bright,
So lively, because
The Sultan of Beauty is among us.

How come this town won't smile
And admire the fact
There there is the gallant
Of time here?

When that sun of beauty
Shines on the world,
The muddy earth
Is better than sky.

Angels with green dresses
Are flying and saying,
"He is our King, our Sultan.
He's worth a hundred worlds."

Give our greeting and tell him,
"O Soul of the Beloved,
Pity the poor.
Your love has no mercy."

How could the world not be green
Since you are the spring?
How could there be no security
If the lion is the guard?

The Soul understood from His smell,
Even before he knocked
On the door of the heart,
That the tender-hearted beloved was coming.

The One who holds your hand
And pulls you is your creator.
The One who is company to your Soul
Is the Sahib Kiran.[15]

He is such a moon, such a sun
That never eclipses;
Such a wine that never gives a hangover.
He is profit without loss.

That great Sultan has set such
An assmbly today that
Candles, wine, and beauty are all free.

When people get drunk,
The real truth comes out.
Then, the one who pretends
To be brave and strong
Is understood by the poor ones.

With the help of the morning breeze,
The rose is separated from the thorn.
Rain is trying to help
The grasses of the garden.

Be silent, let Him talk
Without alphabet or tongue.
If the tongue is His,
What's the use of these tongues?

18.

Verse 2279

"Who is there?" he asked.
"Someone who wants to be your slave,
Your servant," I answered.
"What do you want?" he said.
"O, my moon face, I wanted to greet you."

"How long will you be waiting there?" he asked.
"Until you accept me."
"How long will you be exuberant?"
"Until the day of resurrection." I said

I have sworn, saying,
"I got involved with that business of love.
I made an oath. I lost all my belongings,
My name, my reputation,
Because of Love."

"The judge would ask a witness," he said.
"My tears are my witnesses.
My pale face is my evidence," I answered.

He said, "Your witness is not acceptable;
It comes to eye, he has no good reputation.
He is involved in many bad things."
"I swear, your great Honor," I said.
"They both are innocent,
They both are just."

"Who was your company," he asked,
"While you were coming here?"
"Your spectre." I said. "Your spectre, my Sultan."
"Alright," he said. "Who called you here?"
"The smell of your glass," I said.

"What is your intention?" he asked.
"I want to be a loyal lover."
"What do you want from me?" he asked.
"The favor. I want the favor
You give to everybody and everything," I said.

"Where is that most beautiful one?" he asked.
"In the palace of the Kayser," I said.[16]
"What did you see there?" he asked.
"Many kindnesses. Many favors," I said.

"Why is the road so empty?"
"From fear of the brigand," I said.
"Who is the brigand?" he asked.
"That blame, that reproach," I answered.

"Where is a safe place?" he asked.
"Devoutness and withdrawal," I said.
"What is devoutness?" he asked.
"The road to happiness." I answered.

"Where is disaster?" he asked.
"Around your love," I said.
"What kind of shape are you in there?" he asked.
"I am with exact truth there," I said.

Be silent.
If I keep telling His witticisms,
You will go out of yourself.
You will have neither door nor roof.

19.

Verse 2291

Every moment he brings greetings.
Says, "This letter is from so and so,"
As if greeting and paper are
Very expensive in our town.

No dwarf has ever received
A free kiss from any beauty with that trick.
It is only the male donkey
Who puts out his nose and sniffs.

Whoever has money and wealth,
That silver statue of beauty is there.
Don't keep saying "My soul, my world."
That soul will fly away from you.

You scratch the mine with your finger.
Do whatever is necessary.
Just obtain the gold and then don't hide it;
Because if gold is hidden,
The beauty doesn't appear.

If it wasn't gold, the earring
Wouldn't be put on the ear.
The earring will tell
The importance of the person who uses it.

Even if you don't have
Gold, silver, or money,
Still try to get a beauty.
Somehow, by chance, that kingdom
Will come into your hand.

But this Beloved can't be bought with gold.
You offer him a soul
Which looks like gold.
Dead gold won't do much there.

Gold is nothing but ordinary stone.
There, a kind of stone is split in half
And the seed of instigation is inserted.
Anyone who is after minted gold
Is a raw charlatan.

Be silent.
Once love comes in one place,
Words become worthless.
Be silent so you won't be worse than gold:
Because the Beloved also has no tongue.
He is silent.

20.

Verse 2300

I accept every cruelty
That comes from you
As a favor to my soul.
I hang my neck with my own guilt.

O, moon-faced Beauty,
Your hundreds of cruelties
Are like clothes made
Of material valuable to the body,
Happiness for the soul.

Everybody in this universe
Has his share from You.
Mine is Your love.
It is wonderful. You gave me that.

Because of the taste of Your wine,
Sometimes the glass becomes drunk.
Sometimes the wine overflows
Because of the taste of Your glass.

Meanings prostrate as soon as they see Your face.
Every alphabet starts dancing
As soon as it hears Your words.

When the lover becomes too drunk,
He starts blaming himself
Because to be blamed
Is the appetizer for wine.

21.

Verse 2306

They put you in their eyes
Because of your greatness.
They gave you a place in their eyes,
Then, see, they've all gone
And left you alone at the end.

O, Joseph, your untrustworthy
Brothers sold you.
They sold you cheap, lowered your price.

The ones who have seen
The unfaithfulness of this world
Have already left the living
And gone.

You have so many secret enemies
You don't see them.
You have tried every trick,
But they defeat you in the end.

The invisible Sultans have seen that.
Because of their love for you,
They all pray for you.

Stay with the ones who have space in the heart.
The ones who have a grudge against you
Turn you into a new student.
You don't have hands or feet.

These are the hidden ones.
The others are masters of the servants.
They set a trap and bend you
Like a harp, suddenly.

Be afraid of them.
They know your thoughts.
And others have no loyalty.
See, they did the same thing to you.

22.

Verse 2314

A house full of drunks.
Even then, more drunks came.
All the crazies broke their chains.

We have been very careful.
Took every measure so they wouldn't hear us.
But fate announced an accident like a drumbeat.
They all heard the sound of the drum.

All the souls of the drunks,
And hearts of lovers,
Broke from their cages
And flew away like birds.

Yesterday, I came from a journey
And met that kind of crowd.
I tried to stay away from them,
But they pulled me to themselves.

The only eyes which could see the soul
And the One who chooses the sky for a house,
Is the talented one who has an inside view.

A cupbearer came forward,
Spread all kinds of instigation to the sky,
Created all kinds of commotion.
Since then, the wine is overflowing and pungent.
That's why they tear the skin of its bag.

Drunks broke the jars,
Sat in the cellar.
My god, what kind of wine
Did they drink, and what did they eat?

23.

Verse 2321

The sea doesn't need fish.
Fish are just ordinary
Creatures for the sea.

You cannot find fish
In the endless sea.
But there are many fish
In God's sea.

The sea resembles a nanny.
Fish are like nursing babies,
Keep crying for milk like hungry babies.

If this indifferent sea feels
Some attraction toward the fish,
This is a great favor
And kindness for the fish.

There is a fish which the whole sea wants.
Whoever knows this fish,
Understands his greatness
And will step on Esir.[17]

The sea doesn't care for anything
Except when this fish points out
Or directs something.
The sea will react and follow him.

The fish who receives this favor
Is like a Sultan.
And that endless sea is his minister.

If anyone dares to call him a fish,
Every drop of the sea
Becomes an arrow and destroys him.

For how long will you
Be speaking in symbols?
Your symbols confuse the people.
Speak openly, so the eyes of the heart
Will see and understand.

Shemseddin, whom everybody serves,
Is master and protector.
Because of him, Tebriz
Turned into musk and ambergris.

If the thorns of the world
Received his favor,
They would become as silk
For softness and grace.

I would lose my soul,
If my soul was aware of itself,
With his wine
And the drunkenness of his beauty.

24.

Verse 2333

The one who is sick with a bile disorder
Would not know the taste of sugar.
Every stone-hearted one
Couldn't tell pearls from stones on his way.

The spider that is busy making its web
Wouldn't have any pleasure
Besides that of making a spider web.

The one who lost his position, his job,
Will get into wine, hold the glasses.
He gets so drunk that he couldn't
Differentiate his head from his feet.

25.

Verse 2336

This is a wonderful time.
What we need now is wine.
At a time like this,
We would give our soul
Just to drink a cup of wine.

Our wine comes from the jar of Absence,
The place where we set our assembly
Is at the great throne of God.

Wherever you see a poor one,
Stay with him.
Avoid the fortune teller, the witch doctor.

But stay away from the poor
Who are fond of food.
We need a poor one like Beyazid[18]
Who became poor by giving up
His belongings, his Being.

The one who was born from
Cleanliness and brightness,
Looks for clean.
The one from the dirty, needs dirt.[19]

Fake and real gold sometimes look the same.
But they are differentiated
Under the light of God.

God put a lock on the heart and sealed it.[20]
You have to struggle in grief
In order to open it.

It doesn't matter to the donkey
If the door is locked.
It falls asleep outside.
But the one in the house
Has to open the lock in order to go outside.

Only the ignorant celebrate
Two holidays in a year.[21]
We are Sufis on a journey.
There are two holidays in every moment for us.

The soul says, "I am newborn with your order."
New sustenance is necessary for the newborn.

Fresh daily bread comes to us
From the place of Salvation and Union.
Naturally, dry bone for the ones not new.

O one who comes to the assembly of Sema
Like a cypress,
Death should come to life.
Lifeless personalities should be enlivened now.

If you are a dead, dry branch,
You have to go in the fire.
But if you are a green branch,
You'll come up with leaves and fruits
And bend down.

You reached the pleasure that comes
Flowing to the breast of the mother.
He put this into your mouth,
You must suck it.

You have spent your whole life
With elegant speeches.
For some time you should
Walk alone in the gardens of silence.

Oh, God's sun, Shems of Tebriz,
You are the one who attracted me to words.
You made me talk.
I should breathe for two days
In the world of silence.

26.

Verse 2352

What else could come out of sugar
But kindness and sweetness?
What else could the moon do
But lighten the sky?

What else would be in the rose garden
But heart-catching colors?
What else could grow in fresh branches
But leaves and flowers?

What can you find in the star of Jupiter
But good luck?
What else could be found in a gold mine
But shining gold?

What could the bright sun
Give to the ruby?
What shape can a lung become
From the fountain of life?

What would happen to the eye
That sees the beautiful One
Who created beauty?
See and understand what would happen
To your sight, once you looked at God.

We gave ourselves to exuberance.
To drunkenness, to the worship of beauty.
As long as we live,
What else could come from us?
What can we do?

There is a trace of Being left in us.
Be brave, cupbearer. Give that red wine.
Is there any talk more brief than that?

You are drunk, be more drunk.
No up, no down would be left for you.
Go beyond yourself, know nothing.
What comes out of knowledge, anyway?

Let's go out with rose-colored dresses, like roses.
Let's be crazy, insane.
What's in sleep?
What's in food and drink?

O, Sultan Selahaddin, don't leave that form.
Don't go away from this world.
Show the angel what is in man.

27.

Verse 2362

After Sema, you said,
"What has happened to all the exuberance;
Our flowing excesses?
Where did they go?"
Just like nothing has happened.

Don't deny it. Look at the staff of Moses.
It was a staff once,
And became a dragon afterward.

The body resembles a dragon with closed lips.
But in reality, he swallowed the whole universe,
Then turned into a staff.

A pearl of egg size became exuberant,
Then melted, turned into sea.
Its waves made the earth.
Its vapors, the sky.

Really, a secret cavalry,
Dressed like a Sultan
Comes and attacks every moment,
Then goes back to its origin.

He just went to another world,
Which is hidden from us.
That doesn't mean he doesn't exist.

All behavior is like arrows
At the bow of the body.
When they leave the bow,
They are directed to the target.

A shell grabs a drop of water
And disappears.
But a good diver knows
Where to look for that drop.

Blood boils because of
The love of man and woman,
And becomes sperm, ovum.
Then a tent is set in the sky
From these two drops.

After the soldier of man came
From the land of soul,
Mind became the minister.
Heart is the Sultan and sits at the throne.

After a while, heart missed
The town of soul and returned there.
The rest of the army
Went back to the land of existence.

If you ask how senses come and go,
Pay attention to the time
Just before you fall asleep.
That period will explain many things for you.

The following verses are in "Güldeste."

Organs are like laborers.
They do different things in different places.
The heart is their controller.
They all work under Him.

I won't tell you all these activities.
I will keep silent now.
Fate's back is bent because of His sorrow.

My heart, my soul, my body
Are shining from the reflection
Of the light of Shems of Tebriz on my heart.

28.

Verse 2374

What would happen if you
Gave up thought for one moment,
Plunged into our sea like fish,
And swallowed the waves there?

If you sleep from your thoughts,
Give them up.
You will be one of the Ashab-i Kehf
And turn into a holy light,
Exempt from thought.
Why don't you become like this?

You are a piece of straw.
We are stately amber.
Why don't you slip out
Of this earth and turn into amber?

You promised a hundred times
To become Earth.
Why don't you keep your promise this time?

You are a hidden pearl.
But look to be the color of the soil in this barn.
O Beautiful one, why don't you
Wash all that dirt from your face?

You are the Son of the Sultan.
Even Gabriel prostrates in front of you.
What wonderous things would happen, oh poor one,
If you looked for your Father's land?

O, one who thinks that
Saints and friends of God
Are different than God,
Why don't you have
A better idea about Saints?

You are a fragment,
Separated from the whole,
Hand out of body.
Why don't you stay with us from now on?

Then you won't have a head.
You'll lose your belongings,
Be out of ambition and pride.
But at the same time, you appear
At the land of greatness and are seen.
Why don't you do that?

Drink some juice from God's praise
And be saved from thought.
O, one who is honored by God's consent,
Why don't you stay out of struggles?

It is enough. You look like a mountain.
Search the gold mine in the mountain.
Don't make noise so the mountain echoes you.

29.

Verse 2385

This soul is like a glass.
How does the soul know that?
It is filled by someone very clean
And the glass empties its contents
To the man who is made of earth.

The glass is busy with its work constantly.
It takes from the Throne of God
And spreads to the Earth.

It doesn't know the place
Where it is serving.
It would be nice if it knew the place
From whence it was taking.

The Earth is shining like a mine
To give its blessing to souls.
It they could talk,
Would they give us epigrams?

If they could talk,
They would say the same thing
About that forest, that eternal forest.
What would this forest offer to our soul?

Here, the tiger yells and shouts, "Yâ hû."
The gazelle is asking, "O shelter of sighs,
Who is pulling and dragging us?"

Such a lion, that gives nothing
To our existence but his own milk.
Free Self from ourselves, from our being.

That lion shows himself to us as a gazelle,
And pulls us to the forest with that trick.

Sometimes he gives us Fatiha,[22]
Gives us abundance.
Sometimes he gives us only
A piece of straw, lowers us.
But when we become Fatiha,
He hesitates, doesn't even read us.

30.

Verse 2394

The glorious sun
Has appeared in the sky again,
Raised from the peace of dawn.
The wishes of the souls come again
From the way of the Soul.

With the permission of Ridvan,[23]
The doors of heaven are opened.
Every soul plunged in the pool
Of Kevser up to his neck.

That Sultan came again
Who is Kible to the Sultans.
That moon came again,
Which is greater and better than the moon.

The ones who are dizzy with love
Ride their horses
Because that peerless, unique rider
Came to the center, the heart of the army.

Eyes of all
The particles of black soil are blurred, admired.
Hear the call from the land of Absence,
"Get up, it is time for the last day of judgment."

This unconditional voice is not
Coming from inside nor out,
Neither from the left nor right.
It is not from the back nor the front.

"Alright," you say. "Where is that side?"
The side which has been kept searching.
"Where shall I turn my face?" you say.
From wherever that head comes.

It's the side where ripeness comes to fruit,
The side where the stone becomes a jewel.

The side that, with its abundance,
Brought to life the cooked fish in front of Hizir.[24]
The side from which favor comes
Turned the hand of Moses
Into a shiny moon.

That fire was borne on our hearts
Like a full moon.
This judgment was put on our head
Like a crown.

The soul doesn't have permission
To talk about that.
If he ever talks, all disbelievers
Will be saved from doubt.

Even the disbeliever turns to this side
In difficult times.
When he has problems on this side,
He believes in the other side.

Suffer. Suffer that.
The suffering guides you,
Takes you toward that side.
The only one to see this side
Is the one who is frustrated from troubles.

The greatest of the great Sultans,
Dressed with a human mantle today,
Came through locked doors.

31.

Verse 2408

The bird which was in our trap
Suddenly broke all the traps
And flew to the land of Absence.

The meaningless, ordinary wine
Has been purified.
It's become the purest of the pure;
Has overflowed from the troubles
Of the two worlds, fermented.
Sediment went down deep, and
The wine came to the surface of the jar.

Heart has cleansed this Soul
From the Earth, then ascended
And found a better abode there.

He found many sweet pleasures
In that land of freshness and brightness.
His face became pale like saffron
By describing the tulip faces.

Whoever hasn't met that moon,
Whoever cannot read this form and design,
This writing of His Beauty,
Only stays at the level of religious designs.
I swear to God, he becomes unfaithful.

I have given up my epithets.
I have undressed myself,
Become stark naked.
The sun is the only
Cover for the naked.

It is not nice to say "God is Great,"
While one is still in the world of existence.
When this head is sacrificed,
Then "God is Great" words
Become reality,
The real essence of God manifest.

Greatness is far away from the Soul,
Which gets easily wearied.
If you are bored with love,
Your ship stops sailing and is anchored.

O, God's Sun, Shems of Tebriz,
Heart has fallen in the abyss
In front of your sun,
And has become so small,
Has become more worthless than
Even the smallest of the small particles;
Has turned into nothing.

32.

Verse 2417

Get angry with the one
You can get away from;
The one you don't need,
The one you don't expect to hold your hand
And help. Accept the ground under your feet.

Assuming you let him go, you left him.
You are the king. Nobody is like you.
But, for sure, the day will come
When Death will stand in front of you
Like a master.

You are superior, peerless,
And drink from the Fountain of Life, like Hizir.
The one who doesn't drink His water
Will be in the trap of death.

O, Master of the Soul of creation!
O, Master who is not an illusion!
The One who appears in reality,
Not the one who gets old;
The one whose hair becomes milk-white.

O, Master, don't be a master
To the one who pretends
To be master to the real Master
With deceit, lies and insolence.

Be Master to the one who
Dies for you.
Becomes humble for your greatness.

How can the sun appear as a circle
To the one who sees the hair
Of his eyebrows as a new moon?

How can the one who swaggers
Constantly because of his greatness
Be enlightened by the light of greatness?

O, wealthy one, don't show
Off your possessions.
Annihilate yourself
So that the particles of your existence
Become the sun.

Put a dam to those black torrents,
To block and protect the five senses.
At the end, universal intelligence will
Rain mercy from six directions.

If you don't put the yeast
Of that dough to your flesh,
Even if you cook a hundred years
In the oven, the bread
Won't be ready.

Be straight, like an arrow,
If you want to approach
"Two bows distance."[25]
Only the one who gets into His bow,
The one who looks like an arrow,
Will be thrown to the target.

Be silent!
Say the meaning without the alphabet
If you can.
Say it without words, so the heart
Can take over the conversation.

33.

Verse 2430

Welcome. The holiday is here.
The Beloved, who attracts
Hearts, has come.
The dead jump out of the grave
And come to His temple.

The word came to Heart
To invite the Soul to war.
That friend came to the front.
Soul will come by dragging his feet.

The soul has been submerged
In honey and sugar from the fountain.
The moon has fallen on the harvest
And is surrounded by a halo
From that Turk who resembles the moon.

The soul has become Kible
To the angels, because of
The light of his breath.
Even water resembles fire
If it stays close to the fire.

The heart and souls of the angels
Come so close to God
That the sky becomes a carpet, a cover
To the angels.

Be brave.
Polish the mirror of your heart
And read all the writing
And designs reflected there.
Six directions are also filled
With a variety of designs and
Writings without signs and designs.

You will find that garnet
In your bosom.
Its light spreads to
The heart of the pure person.

He became drunk and fell asleep
From the opium of Bidat's sherbet.[26]
The kingdom has set a throne and seat
At the top of the pole of Mercy.

How smart is that ear,
That His hand held and pulled?
How clean and honest is that face
Which He has scratched?

Be silent.
Listen to the turns
Of the five times of the sky,
Which is beyond the five senses
And the six directions.

34.

Verse 2440

Rise, jump, wake up from sleep.
Bright daylight has come.
Pull your heart from sleep.
It is time to go.

All these signs keep coming.
How long will you ignore them?
I am afraid love will say,
"This Hodja is getting senile,
Becoming an imbecile."

All the gleaners are gone.
This one is left to sit here.
He has become so heavy, so soft,
He turned into a heap of grain.

35.

Verse 2443

O, Lovers, the moon that exceeds
Everybody's beauty is sending messages to you.

He wrote a line on the roll
Of paper of the sky.
Whoever knows how to read
Comes and reads that line.

That line is the secret
Of Soul, written by saffron.
Every word is a blazing fire,
Burning the heart.

We took refuge in one corner,
Fell in love, wore a patched mantle.
Where are we? Where are the people?
But He grabbed our necks and kept pulling.

We are like a ball, armless, footless,
Rolling over in His direction.
His hair is like a club which
Keeps us running that way.

If I run in this direction,
His club hits me to His side.
Tell me, who knows this secret?

Wherever I am, I am drunk.
I worship His club.
Until He asserts His authority,
I exist in the middle of Absence
Or as I appear, as I exist.

Because you are tired and bored,
Go to sleep.
Put your head down,
Conform with the sleeper.
Because sleep saves the one
Who is cold and frozen.

If my Shems shows up,
Comes forward from Tebriz,
I swear to God that no dregs,
No trouble, will remain in two worlds.

36.

Verse 2452

Will it be any cause for decision in the heart
If we see your drunk eyes?
Stars won't be counted if your face,
Which resembles the moon, should be seen.

When your pleasure's player starts
Playing the harps of joy,
It won't be any gain or loss
For Venus up in the sky.

No town or country will remain
If the commanders of Yagma,[27]
For your beauty,
March their soldiers in that direction.

If your rose garden,
Which adds Soul to souls,
Smiles on the garden of soul,
The roses lose their minds
And thorns lose their sharpness.

Once the spy of your love,
Who resembles the Sultan,
Enters the heart,
Nobody finds a place but love.

What a happy, joyful time it is
When, with good luck, You suddenly
Take the Soul in Your arms
And cast the body aside.

Such drunkenness comes to the head
From such Beauty,
That the heart doesn't look for a crown or throne.
Shame and bashfulness go away.

I beg God that
God's Sun, Shems of Tebriz,
Rises to the cave of heart
And stays there with his friend.

37.

Verse 2460

O charmer, whose temple of beauty
Can only be visited by noble houris,
Is it fair that grief will get
In the house of your image?
Is it suitable for grief to stay there?

Every Being is from You.
You are the origin of existence.
The only thing for us to do
Is annihilate ourselves in Your Being.

O, Grief, pull yourself together.
Here, there is an army of joy.
Keykubad,[28] king of joy, is coming
To this country with hundreds of flags.

Don't worry, O heart.
Right now a harp is coming.
A harp which is full of melody
But which is empty inside.

That cupbearer who belongs to God
Is coming from the assembly of the Sultan.
The player of meanings
Will start the melodies now.

O, Grief, how insolent you are.
You are such a desperate one,
Still trying to force yourself in my door.

At last, O Grief, I will submit myself
To the One who adds Soul to soul,
And be free from your fire.

38.

Verse 2467

One has to be alive in love.
Death is no good.
Do you know which one is alive?
The one who is borne by love.

The anger of roaring lions,
And the bravery of all men,
Are nothing to love.

There are some who stage a hold-up on the road.
These fellow travelers are women.
Their feet are dyed with henna
And are not good for this road.
They cannot complete the journey.

War drums are beating to invite
The great Rustem[29] to fight.
A big army is gathered with the invitation of love.

His thunder comes from the heart.
His soul flashes like lightning from the body.
But he doesn't stay the same for even one moment.

The sword of death cannot cut a head like that.
Because his head is so great
That it touches the Throne of God.

A heart like that doesn't contain
Any grief or sorrow.
Earthly grief increases his joy.

Don't believe it if you see him looking angry.
He resembles the clouds of spring.
The whole world smiles and becomes sweet with him.
He does this as a joke;
Pretends to look angry.

The gazelle doesn't look for the lion.
Its lion is Him.
Disbelievers eat lots of grass,
Chew lots of thorns in this pasture.

Look for us in love,
And for love in us.
Sometimes I praise love.
At other times, love praises me.

When he opens his mouth
Like a shell in the ocean,
He swallows the sea of me and us
Like a single drop.

39.

Verse 2478

Neither should the eye
Indulge every heart,
Nor the Sultan show his face
To every common person.

However, our contemptible
And despicable ones are different.
He showed them the rose garden,
Saved them from the thorns.

He attracts our dark black smoke
To the light of holiness;
Changes our old devoutness
Into a fully drunk tavern keeper.

He neither gives up nor sells his creatures.
He prepares a crown and throne right here.
But He shows this power
Like a sale in the bazaar.[30]

Humanity is like a lion,
Caged and locked in the Earth's box.
It looks very tired and frustrated.

Once this idle lion roars
And breaks the cage,
Then you can see what he is able to do.

Mohammed and Siddiyk[31]
Appear to be in a cave.
But, in reality, they are in
The seventh level of the sky.

Love is only One,
But it manifests in different forms.
Only, it appears to the eyes of
Cross-eyed illiterates as two or four.

God's Shems is such a sun
That its light reflects on the mirror.
This and that will be able
To see his shadows on the wall.

Whichever tray I open,
The same sweets come from the same sugar.
The shopkeeper is the one
Who shows them differently.

40.

Verse 2488

When I said, "Dear master,
Don't do that. Grief has designs against us,"
He answered, "It is impossible."

How dare grief touch you.
If he goes beyond his boundary,
I will burn and ruin him.

Grief is afraid of us.
He knows us very well.
If he doesn't behave,
I'll put him in the fire
So that billows of smoke will come
From his fire.

Grief knows his enemy and his place.
It is like Earth, and can be
Spread out for the believers.

Since you are with us, from us,
Even if you drink poison,
It will become honey.
It couldn't harm you.

Halil[32] was happy and comfortable
In the fire, in the smoke.
Only God knows that.
He doesn't tell the people
Because they are not dependable.

The one who is trustworthy
Will reach the land of Absence.
Be companion to those of that world.
Similar people accompany each other.

O One whose hands shine
Like the hand of Moses,
I wish Moses wouldn't put his hand
In his pocket.
It would light the world.

Because the rose of happiness
Doesn't grow without Your face, my Master,
Without "We only worship You,"
We only expect help from You.

41.

Verse 2497

*Y*ou ask, "How are you? What do you do?"
There is nothing I can do
While I am with you.
Only wailing and crying will be for me
When I am separated from you."

Even if I drink the wine of heaven
From the golden cup,
The only hangover I get
Is without you.

Whatever I weave is at the loom of your love.
Without you, I swear to God,
There is no woof nor warp to the material.

You look like a river with
No beginning and no end.
The world is like a bridge over this river.
How can one pass this river
With that kind of small bridge?

This world has four seasons,
Each one against the other.
To fight all of them
Leaves no peace, no life for man.

O spring of Beauty,
You come. You are the essence of the seasons.
Come, all the seasons
Will be ended and burnt out.
They all become spring.
Only spring will stay.

42.

Verse 2503

There is a preacher in the pulpit.
He is advisor to himself and
The ones who listen to him.
He is like a spring of water,
Clean and cleanser.

There is one at the pulpit of greatness.
Another one at the lower steps
Who repeats what he hears from above.

Every word is like a world,
Clear as the sky.
He talks in such a way that
It is easy to explain, easy to be understood.

This opens the door to you
From the dark and muddy
Dungeon of the Earth.

He made stairs with the art of language
To the roof of the round sky,
Which kept whirling.

Light is what pulls
The fire out of the wood.
Fire is not something that sparkles
And shines by itself.

Man makes fire by
Hitting iron to stone.
Stars are also created by order,
Following their course of action.

Every prophet brought a brand new miracle.
How is it that miracle doesn't
Spread around, hasn't been recognized?

With that, happy becomes unhappy.
Heaven changes to a dungeon.
Self, because of that, starts lying,
Uses cunning, cheating,
And, at the same time, is cheated.

This pulpit, this preacher
Are all inside of you.
Don't fail to look for them.

43.

Verse 2513

O One who is annihilated in Love
And reaches Absence,
You are Soul beyond Soul.
You have such charm
That it is beyond charm.

You read the secret of the sky,
The condition of this and situation of that
Before it has been written on the board.
You even read more than that.

You keep asking about
The throne of God from the people.
Yet you know all about it, even more.

There is an ocean of Ruby,
Brightest of the bright.
You are a mine of priceless garnet,
And you have many more gems.

You execute the commands given to the Soul
On the day of Elest,
And all the other orders.

That cross-eyed one got confused
At the first step. Saw many from one.
Talked to the first, then the second,
Then saw many and kept talking.

The one who hasn't reached
The world of existence,
Hasn't existed like God's Shems;
Is mortal at the world of truth,
Even worse than that.

44.

Verse 2520

Your face is a beautiful sunny day;
More beautiful than the brightness of the day.
Brighter than the day.
Wine is good, but the cupbearer
Is better than the wine.

Every hidden thing opens today.
The heart reaches endless wishes.
Like a falcon catching a pigeon.

Every lover gets his deserved
Blessing from the Beloved.
Everyone who is thirsty
Sits by the side of Kevser.

Every moment, the Beloved offers
A new glass and says,
"Today our assembly is open,
Give this to the lovers."

It is such a thin glass that
It appears as if the wine has become the glass.

45.

Verse 2525

O mirror of Absence,
You are Absence, even beyond that.
O one inside of the heart,
You are everything in the heart, even beyond.

You know the secrets of the sky;
Hidden thoughts,
Situations of this and that,
Even beyond.

You read the history of past periods,
The unwritten and written,
To the people, to the angels.
You read even beyond.

You give them their deserved share
From the land of Absence.
You push sorrow out of the heart.
You do many other things,
Many other.

46.

Verse 2529

O one Soul of the Soul of Souls,
You are Soul and even beyond that.
O, chemistry of the mines,
You are the mine and even beyond.

O eternal Sun, O cupbearer of everywhere,
All the coasts, the corners, every store, bazaar,
The disposition of every joy and pleasure,
Are your beauty and charm, even beyond.

O torch for certainty,
For growth and maturity on earth,
Second to the Universal Intelligence, even beyond.

O one who is honored by God,
O light of the Sultan,
What kind of art do you want?
You could do as well, even beyond.

You know things which have no sample,
Everything which has been wondered about,
Every unknown and invisible thing, even beyond.

You make some like Leyla,[33]
Others like Mecnun,[34]
With that love which looks like opium.
O One whose light brightens the sky,
You are something else.

O glory to the chest,
Hope to the patience,
You drag the clouds to the heights,
And do many other things.

O exalted person praised by prophets;
O provision of saints;
O One who builds the house of choice,
You build many other things.

O treasure of mercy,
O sea of pity,
There is no other door on which to rely but yours.
There is nothing beside that anyway.

An eye that sees any other face
To be adorned, besides Yours,
Any other beauty, beside You,
Commits adultery and other wrong things.

O Origin, Beginning of the Beginning,
O helper for tomorrow,
I bend down in the hands of love,
Become something different.

My mouth is full of words,
But I don't talk to anybody but you.
Because other's ears are temporary.
They disappear, even go beyond that.

47.

Verse 2541

O one who frowns in front of me,
You said many bad things about me.
The vulture's mouth smells bad all the time.

The signs of those bad words
Showed on your face.
The ugliness of someone who
Is not good
Appears on his face.

Beloved and Beautiful are ours.
You go and die, eat grief,
Plunge into sorrow.
The sea won't be dirty
Because of the dog's mouth.

If the crusader is filled with hogs,
The name of this holy mosque of Beyt-í Mukaddes
Won't be bad.

This is the face of the mirror.
The beauty of Joseph reflects on this face.
For the stranger,
This is the back of the mirror.

The sun doesn't mind
If bats talk too much.
If the shadow comes reverse to the ground,
The sun doesn't care.

Jesus used to keep smiling.
John the Baptist was very somber.
One smiled because of his confidence in God,
The other frowned because of fear.

They asked God,
"Who is better on this
Already arranged world?"

The one who has a better
Opinion of Me is better.
If the guilty has a good opinion,
He'll cleanse himself.

Coming up to you, you are
Neither making a face because of fear,
Nor for the hope of religion.
You frown only because of hate.
Your face is pale, like saffron, with greed.
Blackened from the cheers of the enemy.

Those don't do any good.
Throw them both in the fire.
How sad to the one who saw
The seed of envy in his heart.

Leave him alone.
"His hand would be dry." [35]
This saying is enough for him.
The one who falls in the dark
Is the one who hates the moon.

O Sun, know this very well.
Your enemies are bats,
The other birds are ashamed of them.
Besides, they are caged by darkness.

The one who is the enemy of the sun will perish.
Nothing will remain of him.
If a chip gets into the eye,
How could anybody see or be comfortable?

48.

Verse 2555

Your face is the Soul of Souls.
Don't deprive Soul of this face.
Don't hide in the Earth the thing that is
Bigger and better than Earth.

O Beloved, who is at the pole of sky,
Stays at the sky of the Soul,
You should know that Soul
Turns around you. Make him restless.

Earth became like a smiling pomegranate.
Showed its teeth.
He is uncontrollably impatient.
Calm him down.

His Sun doesn't leave a trace
Of choice for me.
If I have any choice,
What would happen to His?

The wind of love threw me
Around like dust from the ground.
Naturally, where there is wind,
There will be dust.

His spring grows
Everything on the Earth with love.
The seeds have the same hope;
That they become His prisoner in the ground.

The earth, new moon, houris,
Beauty, garden, and sapling
Are all waiting for Him,
Just like me.

Is it His wine? I trust in God.
Is it His trap? God saves us.
Is it His name? O, my God.
I swear to God, nothing is like Him.

I am like roses.
He is my gardener.
My Soul blooms because of Him.
But I will sacrifice this Soul to Him.

I am swaying, about to fall
Like a leaf, but trembling
Lest I fall somewhere other than in his arms.

All his works are trickery.
Bang the cup, tear the curtain.
But not like the vagabond.

He tears my throat.
Shall I tell or not?
You are not the intimate of the secret,
Let Him tear my throat.

49.

Verse 2567

My Beloved has become drunk.
Look at his narcissus eyes.
He starts mumbling,
Starts talking confusedly.

He sways from one side to the other.
It is obvious, he is drunk.

His eyes trouble the drunks,
But don't try to scare us with them.
I am drunk, too.
I am not afraid of the sticks
Of the security men.

O, Love. My God, my God.
The Sultan of Sultans has become drunk.
Jump. Grab his hair.
Pull, bring him over here.

When a thought comes to the heart,
He starts talking about the Beloved.
Then I spread my Soul like hair
To his head. Fill his mouth with gold.

O one whose face opens roses,
O beloved, who talks
Like a singing nightingale,
My God, this gracefulness,
For whom do you do that?

His appearance is all pretext.
He is the light of the sky.
Give up the design of appearance.
His essence is the beautiful one.

With His favor, cold winter
Changes into spring;
Night becomes day.
This dead earth is alive
With His other world.

50.

Verse 2575

If Soul desires anyone but You,
We push him from Self and throw him away.
If skies don't bend their heads for You,
We crush them against each other.

If He asks for his belongings,
We give them to Him.
If He hides in the castles,
We demolish the castles down to earth.

If this world resembles the Soul,
We are the Soul of Soul.
If this sky is like a head,
We are its bright two eyes.

The roots of the tree are the ground,
This sky is its branches and leaves.
The Earth is an olive tree,
We are like its oil.

Since the love of Shems of Tebriz
Is our magnet,
We are iron
On the way to his service.

51.

Verse 2580

His playful eyes told the black hair,
Fallen on his forehead,
I do tricks like so and so.
You grab his hat.

I said to Jacob,
"Joseph is at the bottom of the well.
When he comes to the surface,
Pick him up. Give him a kingdom.
Prosperity."

We show ourselves like pilgrims.
In reality, we are spies for the robbers.
When pilgrims start a journey,
We set the stage to hold them up.

We fool the pathfinders
With the reverse horseshoe and nails.
Like the moon and his army of stars
Reflecting on water in reverse positions.
We are like the branch of the Judas tree,
Which reaches the heights but
Reflects in the water upside-down.

The fox saw a fat tail in the grass.
Told himself, "Isn't it strange?
A prey in the green grass,
Without a trap."

Whereas a wolf fell right down
On the tail in anger.
It didn't even see the trap.

When a fool falls, or gets into trouble,
He says, "That's not my fault."
Isn't his foolishness enough
Fault for him, O brother?

Love also makes a man a fool.
At least, choose a kind of love
That the Beloved's beauty, charm,
And kingdom are worth the foolishness.

If your foot hurts,
Cast a spell to your Soul
And your Soul's foot.
Because this foot is an oxen's foot.
Its spell is only straw.

When your throat is tightened,
You will be relieved by taking a breath.
How can you feel better without sighing?

His love's deed registers "How? What?"
Until you reach the temple of His love.
But when we surrender,
Even the lowest place will be the highest for us.

What beauty that Beautiful one has,
That even forms and shapes
At the work place
Burn our Soul.

I am frustrated trying to figure
What kind of trick or trap
I could use for the one who has been
Taught trickery by God.

The mind helps to find the way
For the one who loses his way.
But what could he do
For the one who lost his mind?

Aren't we men of the Sultan?
We don't want either mind or Soul.
What is mind? His binding.
What is the advice which comes from mind?
What is Soul?
What are his "Hi's" or "Why's"?

Drunkenness is increasing. Be silent.
Never say a word or make a sign,
O, one fearlessly trying to hurt
The one who wants to do him good.

52.

Verse 2596

O one who talks with God's inspiration,
O eyes of truth,
O one who saves people from this sea of fire,
You are an old Master.

There is no beginning of Your beginning.
You are a very great, peerless Sultan.
The one who holds the Soul's hand
And saves him from the disasters
Of the world's attachments.

You are the One who catches the Soul
When death releases it.
I wonder whose Soul, among the preys',
Is the one deserving to be caught.

Who is the creature that could
Talk about your love?
Even the Glory of God is in love
With your face, your beauty.

I have been caught up in this love.
I have been sick with this love.
I cry. I wail. O, good doctor,
What do you advise me to do?

Your favor asks me to come.
Your grief says to go back.
Which one is true among these?

O Sun of Soul, O God's Shems of Tebriz,
Every particle turned into a Soul
With your light and
Became graceful and talkative.

53.

Verse 2603

I haven't seen any joy,
Pleasure, or music in both worlds
Besides you, O Beloved.
I have seen many wonderful things,
But I haven't seen anyone like you.

I was told that fire
Is for the unbelievers.
They are the ones who burn with it.
But I haven't seen anyone
Deprived of your fire but Abu-Lehib.[36]

I put my ear on the window of heart.
I listened a long time.
I have heard many words,
But I haven't seen the lips that speak them.

Suddenly you blessed this
Humble servant of yours.
I haven't found any reason for that
Except unaccountable favors.

O choice cupbearer,
O apple of my eye,
A beauty like you came
Neither from the land of Acem,[37]
Nor from among the Arabs.

Pour the wine from glass that
Cannot be found, even in Alepo;[38]
The wine that doesn't come to the trough
When it is crushed.

Serve so much that I will come down
From the horse of existence
And walk on foot;
For I see nothing but fatigue
When I am sober.

You are the Sun.
You are the Moon.
Honey is you. So is sugar.
You are the mother and father.
I have had no family but you.

O love which doesn't allow
One to fall into destitution,
O place where God
Looks and is Manifest,
You are shelter and support.
I haven't found a nickname,
A word, to describe you.

We are pieces of iron.
Your love is the magnet.
You are the source of desire,
Though I haven't seen any desire in you.

Brother, be silent. Leave these matters
Of manners, knowledge, and talent.
The more you talk about manners,
The less I see in you.

O God's Shems of Tebriz,
O the one essence of the Souls,
I haven't seen fresh dates
Without your Basra's[39] date of existence.

54.

Verse 2615

O player, sing this Gazel.
I gave up my Beloved and
All kinds of roses and thorns.
I vow not to do it again.

I was either drunk, or sleepy and languid.
I gave up that business.
I vow not to do such business again.

I was down deep, up to my neck
In the sin of repentance.
Now, I repent all the repentances
I have made in the past.

O you who sells wine in this village,
O cupbearer, give me the biggest jar.
I gave up honor. I repent the shame.

I resemble a fallen drunk.
I am out of four natural qualities.
I repent hot and cold, wet and dry.
Gave up all four of these.

My heart has been torn to pieces
Looking for help.
When I understood that helplessness
Is the only help, I repent helplessly.

Enlighten this dark night.
Show your moon face.
I repent so much
With the pleasure of that sin.

I said, "It is time to repent."
A lover answered me,
"I did yesterday.
I am an older repentant."

The one who denies the land
Of Selahaddin's yakiyn,[40]
Who says with love,
"I repent denials."

55.

Verse 2624

O sky that seeks my fault,
O roof that is full
Of noise and fights,
How long must I hide
From your trickery?

O fate, the one which sucks people's blood,
I am a cloud that looks like blood.
Why shouldn't I rain blood on your head?

Heart, keep burning nicely.
Don't try to flee from those two fires.
They are good for you.
Your Soul is mixed with love.
You need love.

Intention is like a light.
The universe is the oven.
This love resembles the fire.
People are the wood.

I cheerfully plunged, like a moth,
And sat in the middle of the fire,
The way God's Abraham did.
I cannot get up from there.

56.

Verse 2629

The sound of the Beauty
Came right from my Soul.
When I heard that,
I ran to your love like the wind,
Like water, like fire.

The ones who were watching
The beauty of Joseph cut their hands.
Put your hand in our Soul.
See what we cut?

The situations of the penniless
And rints[41] are obvious.
What else is left?
We also put this torn mantle
In front of your feet.

There are many like us,
Who give their Souls to the land of Love.
But we haven't seen anyone
Like you. Even in a dream.

We were frightened,
Seeing our shadow on the water
Like animals, while drinking water.

57.

Verse 2634

Yes, while I struggle, insist,
You are fighting back.
But I am not that weak,
That frustrated yet. I won't run.

You didn't come to me.
Pretended to be asleep.
If you sleep, I swear
I'll pour this wine on you.

O, great happiness,
Give me the glass.
Don't try to send me back quickly.
I won't get up from my place that fast.

Your face says, "I am the light
That illuminates every moment."
Your hair, "I am the belly button
Which drops musk all the time."

O Beauty, whose skin is like jasmine,
I won't settle for less than eighteen glasses.[42]
Be nice, be easy, O tough, stern Beauty.

O favor beyond boundary,
Hug me nicely. It would be so nice
To resurrect on the last day
If I die in your arms.

Offer wine. Quit this joking, being playful.
I am not after the bride's trousseau.
I am drunk for the bride.

I want to have a wine like fire,
Like a pomegranate.
You'll push a big kettle in front of me.
How long will I turn around this kettle?
Am I a skimmer?

I am not like a braying donkey,
Nor in love with urine.
O friend Jesus, give me
The wine of monks.

Be silent! If you are not a hypocrite,
Listen to love.
I am the friend of Rustem,
Not the shameless.

58.

Verse 2644

O One who broke my repentance,
Where shall I run away from You?
O One who settled down, sat on my heart,
Where can I escape from You?

O light of both my eyes,
How could I see without You?
O One who tied my neck,
Where can I escape from You?

O Beautiful One, the lights of your eyes
Turned six dimensions into a six-faced mirror.
O One whose face is blessed,
Where can I escape from You?

Heart is a creature
Which jumped out of You.
Nourished and was nurtured from you.
Soul, on the other hand, is exhausted from You.
Where can I escape from You?

Even if I close my eyes,
You are still in my heart.
You don't go away from there.
Where can I escape from You?

59.

Verse 2649

I came, swaying, to die again
In your presence,
O one who saves me
Again and again from grief and suffering.

I am like the dried, cracked earth.
My cloud is from favor.
My musk is from favor.
I don't want anything but thunder.
I don't take anything in my hand
But your curly hair.

Being your slave is
A hundred times better
Than being free and a king.
Especially when you say,
"O, my sick-hearted slave."

A hand full of dirt that will come
Reaches you better than the gold
Which stays away from you.
Especially the moment you say,
"O, my poor, hungry one."

Leave adventure. Where is the mind
Which will deal with that?
The harp is my ecstasy, my remembrance.
Wine is my sheik, my master.

O Soul of the Soul of drunks,
O one whose hand is treasure for the needy,
I have been engulfed in honey
And milk at the heaven of your beauty.

I have seen the last day of Judgment.
I have lost myself.
My existence has become invisible.
I am bent like a bow,
But I fly like an arrow.

O friend from whom it is impossible
For me to separate,
I was a handful of dust.
The wind coming from you lifted me up
In the air, gave me great height.
But where could I go without you?

O light of my eye, glory of religion,
You said, "Sit down wisely."
O one who tears my curtain,
Are you leaving me alone?

I am the slave of Elest,
I have been yours since then;
But your cruel separation
Is driving me crazy.

How could my tree
Smile without your spring?
How could my dough
Be cooked, if you don't knead it?

Since I have seen your table, your blessing,
I have been saved from crumbs.
Since I have seen your Being,
I am running away from my existence.

I'll lose my mind, my Soul
If you leave me or stay away from me.
I'll climb to the top of the tower of Aeter[43]
If you appear to me;
If you are with me.

O Soul, when I sit at the last ritual
Of prayer, give me a greeting and take mine.
This is the last part of the ritual.
It is not possible without salutation.

How can I stop clapping my hands?
My Beautiful One is in my hand.
How can I stop tapping my feet?
My base tones become high-pitched.
I am upside-down already.

Give our greetings to Shems of Tebriz.
It is good to set a temple to such an East.
I am glorified by the glory of his face.
I want glory from him.

60.

Verse 2665

How can I not be death? Not be crazy?
Not be insane? Not be chained
For such a Beauty who gives Soul?

I drank your wine.
How can I be destroyed?
It looks like you are wine, I am water.
You are honey, I am milk.

Open your mouth. Spread countless sugars.
If you don't listen to excuses,
I'll endure your coyness, your caprices.

Do you understand why I am smiling?
Because of your great zeal.
Because I am the master of lovers
In the city of your love.

I was in the same womb
With everlasting love.
I was born from the same mother.
I am his twin brother.
I swear to God, I'll create a brand new love
Even when I become very old.

You only see yourself with those eyes.
But if you open the eyes of the Soul,
You'll understand there is nobody
Like me.

I fire the ovens of cold people.
In the hot oven,
I am the best-cooked bread
Among the others.

I resemble the milk for drinking.
I don't stay in the throat.
Don't make a wrong judgment
If you find me as salty as cheese.

I am a Sultan with a crown and throne
With the love of Shems of Tebriz.
But if he sits on the throne,
I am a Vizir in his presence.

61.

Verse 2674

I want to boil the kettle
Of the Soul. Spread bloody foam.
I want to say the words of
The two universes in one breath,
In one effort.

I am out of myself.
I became a slave for Love.
I want to make all the universe
Go out of itself.

I twist the rope girdle
Of bad self around his neck.
He says, "When I scream
I'll be free and fly away."

But how could he be free?
I will pull in such a way that
He will turn all around the world.
His smoke-colored Soul will
Be engulfed in fire.

I will snatch the veil
From the face of the bride of Soul.
I will deprive the ones who are the leaders of love
Of wealth and property.

I'll make this Earth a harp of Love.
I'll make three hundred languages
Out of this mute harp.

Shems of Tebriz stretched such a bow
At the land of love that,
When I let go, not only the arrow
But the bowstring will fly away.

62.

Verse 2681

You're hiding your heart from me.
Pretending you don't know.
You are mixing all the words
And alphabet together, like saying
You don't know how to write.

I am the one who wrote
All those things on your imagination.
How can I not know the secret
Of your heart?
I am inside of your Soul.

I am better and brighter than the sun.
Particles of Souls are dancing in front of me.
They all turn toward my temple,
Where I scattered pearls.

How could particles be visible
Without sunshine?
O atoms, how can you stay
Away from my gravity?

Earth has been turning
Around my light like a moth.
I am the one who burns its wings.

This cracking up, piece by piece;
This indescribable love,
Is union with the Beloved.
If you want to understand love,
I'll take you to His presence.

If you are in doubt, make sure
The doubt comes from me to you.
I draw down deep the one
Who denies with that trick.

If you are faithful,
This also comes from me.
I catch the ones who are at the top
With the same net.
Save them from blasphemy.

If you have any grief, any trouble,
Find me in this grief. See me in this trouble.
Because the arrow of distress
Flys out from my bow.

When difficulty turns into comfort,
When arrows become shields, pay attention.
This also comes from my favors.
This is a gift for you.

Wherever this beauty exists,
Relations are alright there.
But I cannot talk
Where the master of greatness exists.

63.

Verse 26092

Give us wine constantly
So we will be together, become one.
For just one moment,
Throw away our forms.

If we give ourselves up,
We will all have the color of the same water.
We are branches of the same tree.
We are all neighbors.

We have the same character of love.
Hidden, at the same time obvious.
We are hidden at the city of love,
But wide open at the quarters of love.

If we see ourselves dead,
We go and sit at our grave.
If we see ourselves alive,
We start yelling and screaming,
And tear our faces.

Every shape reflects
On our mirror of heart.
Looks are not bound with anything,
Because we are not bound with anything.

We are a bunch of fish
Walking on the surface of the water.
We throw this ever-changing soil
From one desire to the other,
To the face of Earth.

We have seen the glory of love
Turned into the heart of the penniless.
We had love as cash,
Became merchants without garments.

64.

Verse 2699

I am not myself.
I fell into the world of ecstasy.
There, what a nice joy
And beautiful shape I am in.

In order not to see anyone else,
That Beauty closed my eyes.
At the end, I opened my eyes
And suddenly, I saw Him.

The Soul has started fighting with me.
"Don't hurt me," he said.
"I'll divorce you," I said.
"Go ahead," said he. "I just did."

My mother saw on my face
The mountain on which
Your love is reflected.
Cut my umbilical cord with that love.
I have been in love with you since my birth.

Even though I ride a horse to the sky,
Read the tablet of Absence,
Without you, O One who controls my Soul,
I am in complete defeat and disorder.

O, One who lifts the curtain,
Brings death to life,
I remember the oath of Elest
When I see the holy light of your face.

O Soul, I have been out of myself so much.
I have been hidden from myself,
From people, so much it seems
Like I was born from a fairy.
I almost became one.

I asked my body,
"What are you in front of Shemseddin of Tebriz?"
"Earth," he answered.
My Soul said,
"Someone who is as dizzy as the wind."

65.

Verse 2707

I solemnly promised. I said,
"I broke the bad oath."
He said, "How could you solemnly promise?
How could you break the things I tied?"

I am like honey and milk with Him.
I would hold onto His skirt, but I can't
My hands are broken.

But only the ones whose hands are broken
Can hang onto his skirt.
He cast me down with sorrow and grief.
But now he has lifted me up.

When I go up, His justice
Would put me down.
First I was annihilated,
Then He made me exist again.

O One who has tied
His love-lock on my neck,
Wail from his drunken eyes.
They are the Ones who made me drunk.
Made me drunk.

His drunken image came
Like a drunk attack on me.
I have used every excuse,
But couldn't get away from Him.

I knocked at the door of the Beloved.
"Nobody is here," he said.
That means, "I am here.
Make sure of that."

"Your slave has arrived," I said.
"Those words of yours are a trap," he answered.
"Do you think I'll bite this bait?"

"If you want to burn, burn me.
I deserve it, O Beautiful,
Because I worship such an idol, such a Beauty."

I've become dry so you can burn me good.
If you burn me, I will be saved from fire.

I go wherever you go.
You come wherever I go.
I am happy with you
In life or in death.

O water of vitality, as long as
I am with you, death won't touch me.
I swear to God,
I am saved from death with your help.

66.

Verse 2719

I have died hundreds of times.
I have found this:
Once your smell comes,
I become alive.

I have dropped dead
Hundreds of times.
But once I heard your voice,
I was born again.

I lose myself. I become nothing
When I see your face, O charmer
Who turns me into a feast day and
Burns me like Aloe wood.

I set a trap in my heart
To hunt the falcon of Love.
But he fooled me with many tricks.
Came and snatched me.

O, flame which keeps whirling
The hearts of men,
I turn around your moon
Like the sky.

What a happy moment it was
That I made that oath again and again.
But then I broke them all.
I became the same as I was.

He put the idea in my mind
That I could only reach the Sultan through him.
I went to the side of the mind,
But I couldn't find any help there.

67.

Verse 2726

The ones who denied You
Became the enemy of my drunk Soul.
But Your beauty is the answer for them.

Once you show your face from a distance,
Once you pull the ear of
The one who reproaches you,
I am saved.

I don't believe it if he says,
"Neither pearl nor jewel."
It is not even that, O brother.
I am as I am.

Yesterday, Heart became drunk
Because of the beautiful One.
He became so drunk that I broke
A glass in front of the Sultan.

I am drunk with that Beauty
Whose face is more beautiful than the moon.
I am happy because of that Sin.
I am the culpable one of that Sultan.
Come and break my hand.

I am easy and deceitful.
Belong to the religion of love.
That is why my name is all around.
Who am I to send gifts to the Sultan?

Heart is a thief, a first-class thief,
Waiting in front of the treasure's door.
After I tied the hand of that thief,
The door was opened.

O one who doesn't know that Sultan,
You keep asking, "Where are you?
Where are you going?"
Like a fish in a net,
I go wherever the net pulls me.

God's Shems is my secret,
Tebriz is my supplication.
He is the one, my Kible
At Namaz.[44]   He is the light of my Abdest.[45]

68.

Verse 2735

I am such a dark evening
That I am mad at the moon.
I am such a stark naked, poor one,
That I am mad at the Sultan.

That peerless, unique Beauty
Kindly invited me to his house.
But I am mad at the road of the journey.

If my Beloved is obstinate and coy,
It throws me into grief, makes me helpless.
Even then, I won't say "Ah."
I am even mad at "Ah."

He fools me sometimes with gold.
Sometimes with power and armies.
I am already mad at power.

I am such an iron that
I am running away from the great Magnet.
I am a piece of straw,
Mad at the magnet of the universe.

We are such particles
That we rebel at the four elements,
The fives senses, and the six dimensions.
What are four, five and six?
I am even mad at the only God.

You cannot take this world
Because you are out of the water.
I am getting mad at the ones
Who are like the sun
Because they look like the sun.

69.

Verse 2742

I entered the road of love pure, clean.
I walk on that road, pure, clean.
I don't spread the seeds of grudge.
Even Absence takes shelter in me.
I don't scratch the back of greed.

Neither do I worry about people,
Nor have fear of anyone.
I am a free bird. I don't need
The leftovers of the cages.

I am a raining cloud,
A sky which spreads pearls.
I give the water of life
To the thirsty on the Earth.

It looked like fire to Moses,
But it was the Glory of God
Coming to the heart.
I also look like fire from a distance.
But I am the Glory, O my friend.

The branches of the tree tremble
But its roots stay still.
I may be restless here,
But I settled down at the world of Soul.

I am such a strange universe
That I can be hidden in a handful of dust.
I am light to every night;
Spring to every fall.

I am night for the bird of night;
Day for the bird of day.
But when I come to myself,
I am different from both of them.

I come to myself
When I am totally annihilated,
Out of myself.
I become completed when
I am free from the four elements,
The five senses.

The Soul of man gets
Into an endless dispute of "choice."
His great "choice" took my "choice"
Out of my hand. Left me without choice.

The smart mind has such wind in his head.
But when you offer a glass of wine,
That wind blows away.

70.

Verse 2752

My God, what kind of Beloved have I?
It seems like I have been hunting a lion.
There are hundreds of fields and meadows
In my heart for him to walk and enjoy.

When he comes close to me,
He says, on purpose,
"I have a problem with you.
How long are you going to stay
Away from me?"

Last night, I asked my Beloved
About the new moon. He said
"I have been running after Him.
My feet are full of dirt."

When the sun rose, I asked,
"Why is your face yellow like that?"
He answered, "I saw His face.
I felt so ashamed that my face
Turned into this color."

"O water, you fall down prostrate.
You make your head, feet. You are
Running face down," I said.
He answered, "With His spell,
I keep running and curling like a snake."

"O head of Justice, head of discipline;
O fire, why do you writhe and wriggle," I said.
He answered, "I have such a restless
Heart because of the flame from His face."

"O messenger of the world, the wind,
Why are you so restless?" I asked.
"If I had a choice, never mind restlessness.
My heart would be burned and destroyed," he said.

I said, "O Earth, why are you
In silence? What do you think?
You are in such deep thought."
"Never mind my silence," he said.
"I have gardens and springs inside of me."

Give up all those elements.
God is enough for us.
I have drunkenness in my head.
Wine is in my hand.

If you take my sleep away,
The door of drunkenness is wide open.
For sure, he would serve wine, jar by jar
Since my Beloved's hand is in my hand.

Be silent. That Heart speaks
Without tongue or lips.
When I hear words of the Heart
I am ashamed of words of the mouth.

71.

Verse 2763

O bird in the sky,
It is time to fly.
O gazelle of meaning,
It is time to spread musk.

O unique lover,
O one who was chosen among the lovers,
It is time to give up "created."
Watch creation. See the Creator.

Enlightenment has come to you.
You are Soul. Such a Soul,
Who knows to run like a specter
Through the eyes.

Orders come now.
They will teach you
To see without eyes,
Hear without ears.

He knows how to curl a mustache;
At the same time, to bring the dead to life.
He knows how to give the throne of destiny;
At the same time, to educate and bring up humans.

Even the Joseph of Meaning,
That free treasure, lowers his price.
But I wonder if you know how to buy him?

Where is that customer who knows
How to tune in two different notes
At the same time; tear the fret
Of the stringed instrument?

O successful lover,
O one who has been proven,
You should turn around your own pivot,
Like the sky.

Search for yourself in Absence
And find it is difficult
To be contrary or separated from God.

Clean your lips of the devil's milk.
After that, you can drink
From the breast of the heart.

O love of universe,
You keep pulling us.
O one who pulls,
How beautifully you pull.
O one who is pulled,
Bravo for you, too.

The sun knows how to show
Its face from the East.
Otherwise, it is impossible
To reach Him by running,
To know Him by seeing.

Be silent. If it was possible
To tell the conditions of the Heart,
Mountains would start to move
And flutter like the sea.

If you see Shemseddin of Tebriz suddenly,
You can also see the sparks of the wine
Of eternity because of him.

72.

Verse 2777

An army came from the land
Of dark people.
Attacked the center of the army.
O brave one whose head is up,
Attack fearlessly.

Attack like fire.
They are all wood.
With the fire of your heart,
Burn the dry one, burn the wet one.

If the sea starts a war,
Has a grudge with you,
You turn all the waves of hatred into fire.
Destroy all its pearls and coral.

The arrow came from your bow
And pierced the seven layers of sky.
O arrow of state,
Only two distant bows remain.
Attack with His shield.

Put your hand to the head
Of the one who comes headless,
Caress him.
Cut with the dagger the one
Who comes with a head.

The Soul who shines and is enlightened
Keeps burning in your love.
If you want him to regain his freshness
Throw him in the fountain of Kevser.

Make the Earth green
With ruby lips of yours, which give wine.
Take the harp from the hand of Venus,
Throw stones to its glass, break it.

Attack with the power of faith
The infidel Soul of the one
Who denies God's Shems of Tebriz.

73.

Verse 2785

Today, your love brought
All the boasting leaders
To your temple with their necks
Tied with his coyness.

Go. Go to the rose garden.
Watch the ones who worship the rose.
One moment they prostrate,
One moment they drink wine.

That sweet-mannered Beloved
Hasn't left even a piece of hair to us.
That is what shaving the Sufi head means.
Giving up his head.[46]

When you lose your loose tooth,
A new one comes.
Death is the same for the believer.

O enemy of Shems of Tebriz,
O thief who stages hold-ups,
The worst disbeliever;
Shrink yourself, have grief, torture yourself.

74.

Verse 2790

O vain, useless people,
Run, struggle for bread.
O ones who have reached
The kingdom's fortune,
Walk toward the Soul,
Try to get Soul.

Animals pull grass, eat grass,
Don't know anything else.
Humans are the ones
Who search for agates and coral.

Those gardens are asleep,
There is nothing there.
These gardens are open,
Flowers are in bloom.
This is the share for
The palace of the Sultan,
Harvested from these gardens.

There are Souls, far away,
Who haven't reached the Beloved;
Who stay in misery.
There are Souls who have flown, gone,
Who have already reached the Beloved.

There is also a Soul, hard to describe,
Above the sky.
Fine and agile, it looks like
The moon in the sign of Libra.

There is still another Soul,
Hard like fire; rigid, ugly,
Which has a short life.
Looks like the shadow of the devil.

My Hodja, which one are you?
Are you cooked, or still raw?
Are you drunk with wine and snacks,
Or are you only the rider of the field?

One day, while I was traveling
In the valley, I saw a great man.
He was up in the air, dancing
Upward toward the heights.

Everywhere was exuberance
Overflowing because of Him.
But he was very calm, silent.
He was wearing green.
My Soul admired Him.

I asked, "What's this excitement?
You are away from people's illusion.
Are you the glory of the Glory of Glories,
Or a shining sun?"

"My heart was squeezed," He said.
"My body became light as a result of this.
My feet were freed from
The cross of the four elements."

"Master," I said. "How wonderful.
Can I embrace you?"
I begged, begged fervently.
"Impossible," he said.

I said, "Show some sign of faithfulness.
Leave this coyness.
Give me just one sugar cane.
Be generous.
What would be lost from that mine?"

"I am Absent. A reed in the riverbed.
I appear in this form
Just as a remedy for suffering."

"To talk like that is not for You,"
I said. "You can always get rid of me.
O One who speaks well,
Tell me something else."

"How do you believe a one-sided secret
Spoken only from one side?
You are a child," He said.
"Go and learn how to read and write."

I said, "Punish me right away.
It is alright.
Get rid of me with hundreds of excuses.
Kill me with your separation."

Suddenly, He started talking sweetly,
Gave me hundreds of suggestions.
Read all of them by heart.
I was devastated. Became drunk.

I shed many tears.
Stayed there as a drunk for a long time.
Then I saw that Sultan, suddenly come out
Like a Soul in human shape.

A scorch is left on the heart
From this conversation.
A kind of scorch; its pleasure
Worth a thousand favors.

He offered me such unexplainable things.
There was such amazing advice
In those words.
Be silent. It is not easy
To put them into words.

75.

Verse 2811

*L*ook for that Beauty
Here among the beauties.
If someone tells you,
"Don't wake up that troublemaker,"
Don't listen to him.

The Soul smiles with joy
When his image settles the heart.
The suffering of the patient ones
Brings out hundreds of sweet things.

Lights come from his shining face,
Like a full moon reflecting in the eyes.
How could the blind see that?

76.

Verse 2814

O heart, don't run away
From the houri's Sultan;
The Kible of the patient ones;
Like someone who stayed away from him.
Don't excite him.
Don't wake the troublemaker.

I am already someone who looks for trouble.
I can't leave him. I can't give him up.
I can't wash my hands of him.
But don't you excite,
Don't wake the troublemaker.

I am head of the lovers,
Master of wanderers.
I am in love with someone.
But don't you excite,
Don't wake the troublemaker.

Don't ask me how I am,
Look and see yourself.
Drowned in the blood, even worse than that.
But don't stir, don't excite,
Don't wake the troublemaker.

I am Rustem; Soul,
Float for the tribe of Noah,
Drunk from the mornings wine.
Don't wake the troublemaker.

You cannot read this writing
Because you are earthbound.
You only know this much:
Don't excite,
Don't wake the troublemaker.

77.

Verse 2820

O stone-hearted one,
Turn the Soul into a sea full of pearls.
O, the hair of the Beloved looks
Like night. Create dawn in
The middle of the night.

Tune the harp that is played
By heart and Soul with love.
Fill the silent reed with sugar
From the love of that sweet Beauty.

You have hundreds of thousands
Of pearls in your ears and eyes.
Give a handful of them
To the blind and deaf.

Give to lovers the blood
Of heart which smokes,
Smells love as a cup of soup,
Feed them.

Souls have been going different ways
But haven't reached anywhere.
O one who is the answer for Souls,
Teach them a new way.

The wings of birds in water
And in air, got stuck in mud.
O Hüma bird, fly.[47]

Go like the devil. Run around the world.
Find that fairy. Turn your heart
To gold in front of his silvery heart.
Become pale, tired, to reach him.

Signs and orders are coming
From everywhere to you.
To stop asking "why" and "how,"
Walk together with that hot-tempered Beauty.
You beg when he gets more difficult.

Take the Soul that is
Like the feet of an ant
As a gift to His temple,
And wait at every corner
Where the army of Solomon will pass.

The Sea is salty, bitter water,
But there are pearls at the bottom.
You pass through the salty water
And dive for the pearls.

There is a kind of snake
That has an antidote in its head.
If you want to get it,
Pass through the poison.

If you are looking for the tree of Tuba,[48]
Here is God's Shems of Tebriz.
If you look for eternal pleasure, joy, or life,
Sit in the shade of this tree.

78.

Verse 2832

O one who is lost in Absence
On the journey, go even further.
Leave even that behind you.
Look from heart to Heart itself.
See the essence.

Heart is like a Chinese mirror.
If you sit with Heart, you'll see
Hundreds of swords. Don't be afraid.
Make a shield of your eyes,
Put it in front of them.

I know you gave up everything.
You have been annihilated in Heart.
You are right in Absence,
But one more effort is necessary.

Attack once more. Cut your prey
To pieces around this fountain.
Lay a hand on your liver
O lion of the heart.

Since you pawn your carpet
For that peerless pearl,
For one more big test,
Try to put your hand to your belt.

We are particles in sunshine.
Get a little bit of soil
From the particle and put it
On the eye of the moon as salve.

No Soul is left for us
From love and craziness.
O Sultan who sees and knows,
You are the one. Tell us about yourself.

Sweep. Throw away all these forms
And pictures from this earth.
Create a live image of yourself,
O love that resembles fire.

They died, passed away from themselves,
Drank wine. Even that rint
Has greetings for you.
O Sultan, go to their side just one time.

Even the Phoenix would get up
And fly from Kafdagi[49] with the love
Of Shems of Tebriz.
You pull the wing of existence
From its roots. Tear it to pieces.
Get an arm and wing from love.

79.

Verse 2842

A moth, plunging into the fire,
Told me "Do the same."
He was burning, fluttering his wings
And telling me,
"Be like me."

The oil lamp is filled with oil.
Its wick is knotted, burning
With its broken neck,
And at the same time, telling me softly,
"Be like me."

The candle was burning and melting.
It gave itself for heat and suffering.
At the same time, it was telling me,
"Burn and melt like this.
Be like me."

"It isn't worth it to spend
Gold and silver to earn profit
In this world," he was saying.
"Try to burn. Melt this way.
Be like me."

The sea filled his lap with pearls,
Sat at the head, so as not to be conceited;
Showed itself bitter and salty.
It is trying to tell you,
"Be like me."

The Phoenix has given up good and bad,
Is free from traps.
It has settled down on Kafdagi,
Is trying to tell you,
"Be like me."

The rose purified its face,
Tore its robe, enduring the thorns,
Telling you to do and
"Be like me."

Wine gave up hundreds of names
And fame, free from shame and modesty.
Became an enemy to the mind.
Keeps running in man's brain,
Saying to you,
"Be like me."

The shrill pipe became completely empty;
Closed its eyes; only gave its lips
To the one who blows, and was saying
"Be like me."

Adam was in mourning forty years.
Kept crying, telling his children
"Be like me."

Be silent. Learn, at last
A lesson from the hard rock.
It also stays silent, but cries
"Be like me."

See Shemseddin of Tebriz
Fill the valley with the light of Soul;
The plains with greatness, saying
"Be like me."

80.

Verse 2854

Death is the sweetest thing for us,
As long as You take the Soul.
Dying with You is sweeter
Than sweet life for us.

Lift this cover. Don't hide the truth.
Death is like fire, but
For God's Abraham, it is a garden,
The fountain of life.

Death is on this side.
The other side is a birth.
There, nobody dies.
Death is only on this side.

Leave this body, become Soul.
Go to that world with pleasure.
Death is sad and terrible now,
But don't be afraid of death.

I made an oath to the Glory of God,
For whom nine skies became dirt.
That death is like the one who makes
Halva[50] with the sugar of union.

Why should I run away from Soul?
Giving life is Soul. To reach the Soul,
Why should I escape from the mine?
Death is a gold mine.

If you are out of this cage,
You are in the rose garden.
When you break this shell,
Death is the pearl.

When God calls you,
Pulls you to His side,
Going is like Heaven.
Dying is like Kevser.

Death is a mirror.
Your beauty reflects there, appears there.
The mirror keeps telling you
He is the One showing you to yourself.

If you are a believer, a nice person,
Your death is safe, secure, and pleasant.
If you are a disbeliever, a bitter person,
Death is also bitter and bad for you.

If you are like Joseph, beautiful,
Your mirror is also beautiful.
If you are ugly, your mirror
Inevitably shows your ugliness.

Be silent. You are a sweet-tongued
Immortal, like Hizir.[51]
Death is blind and deaf
For the fountain of life.

81.

Verse 2866

O Beloved, make us man first.
Keep us that way, then give us wine.
Keep filling the wine glasses.

O Soul, nothing comes from us
Nor from our temple.
You started building.
You finish it.

You turned our land of happiness
To a land of reproach.
Turn it back
To the land of happiness again.

This endless road is too far, too long.
But, with Your favor,
It is made a two-step road.

You made us hostage to this "Self."
But You are the Master of this Self,
Who orders us to do bad things.
Make us the master, Self the slave.

You give general favors to special ones.
Today, make those special favors
That You give your close ones,
General favors.

Give a new sun to every particle
With Your kindness.
Raise Your sun of favor and kindness
To everyone.

Sweeten the praying for us.
Prayers become like milk and honey
For our mouths.
Favor the one who says "Amen."
Turn him to someone who wants
To do everybody good.

82.

Verse 2874

Look for January's advice.
Stack wood in a big pile.
If the cold doesn't come,
I'll take the blame of the winter and wood.

When the weather gets cold,
Throw wood on the fire.
Trying to save wood?
Is wood better than your health, your body?

Wood is the symbol of Absence.
Fire is the love of God.
O clean Soul, burn forms and shapes.

Your Soul feels frozen if you
Don't burn the forms and shapes.
Stay away from spring and security
As an idol-worshipper.

Fire becomes a rose, tulip, and flower.
Turns into mint and willows
By the order of God.

Plunge into love, which looks like fire.
Keep your heart good, like silver.
Inside of that fire, beautify.
Since you are the son of Abraham,
Fire is your place.

Believers change the fire to a full moon
By the spells they know.
The fire doesn't burn anymore.

Bravo, for that spell
That melts iron to a small needle.

The moth sees fire like a window
And jumps into the flame for that reason.

The arrow and spear look like
A branch of roses for Hamza.[52]
Nobody wears armor against roses.

The Pharaoh went down like yogurt in water,
But Moses stayed above the water, like oil.

Fine horses carry the Sultans.
Dumb, ordinary ones carry only
Saddles and dried dung.

Words are senseless,
Annoying chatter in the mill of meaning.
The millstone turns with water,
Not with chatter.

Because of these senseless words,
Grain jumps out of the tray
And falls under the millstone.
In the other world,
That's the way to be ground.

I am hot, not because of
Gossip or empty words, my friend,
Because of a pure gold mine, like Shemseddin.

83.

Verse 2889

Go, put your head on the pillow.
Leave this sorrowful, burned one
Who walks around all night long.

At night, we struggle through
The wave of love until morning.
If you want, forgive us.
If you want, torture us.

You run away from me
So you'll stay out of trouble.
Be on the way to safety, not grief.

We are suffering at the corner of sorrow,
Shedding tears.
You can run hundreds of mills,
In hundreds of places,
From our flowing tears.

There is someone who is a cruel tyrant,
Who has a marble, granite heart.
He is the One who pulls us.
He would kill man and
Nobody would ask the cost of his blood.

It is not necessary for
The Sultan of Beauty
To be loyal to lovers.
O Lover, whose face turned to pale yellow,
You be patient. You be loyal.

There is a disease
Whose only remedy is death.
How can I ask to find the cure
For that disease?

I saw a master in my dream.
He was at the village of Love.
He signaled with his hand,
Bidding me to come to his side.

He told me "If there is a dragon
On the road, you have love like an emerald.
Go, repel that dragon with
The shine of emerald-like lightning."

Enough. I am not myself anymore.
If you want to increase your knowledge,
Read the stories of Abu-Ali[53] or
The advice of Abu-Ala.[54]

84.

Verse 2899

O, my eyes. It is morning.
Look through my window.
You are the source, the essence of the sun.
Since you came, the dawn is made clear.

Take the ones who desire.
Pass them through seven seas.
Don't look at the oxen and fish,
Go beyond hundreds of them like that.

Find what you are looking for.
Bring up what you search for.
You are free from all creatures.
Turn this old house upside-down.

The universe is nothing but Absence.
You make it exist in one moment.
A poisonous snake is this world.
Try to change this poison into sugar.

Wherever you see a dryness,
Make a running spring.
Wherever you see a stone,
Shine on it, make it a jewel.

If you see an enemy
In front of or behind the lover,
Slap him, destroy him.

How long will you give
Excuses as they are?
The blind cannot see.
Give them the power to see
If you don't want them to be blind.

If you don't want curtains
Over their eyes, give orders
For the curtains to be lifted,
So they won't be blind anymore.

Among all these crowds,
Command is absolutely yours.
I folded the Kaftan of idleness
Rose and ordered, "Put on the belt of zeal."

O Sun of the Throne of God,
O God's Sun of Tebriz,
I am pale and weak like a new moon.
Turn my face into a full moon.

85.

Verse 2909

You asked, "How are you?"
Look at our face.
You'll understand how we are.
Were you alright when I was gone?
Never mind this sarcasm.

You said with a smile,
"Have a good day."
If you are not around,
Nobody has a good time.
Tell me another story.

"I am tired of how long
You keep talking about love," you said.
Tell that to the one who is not in love.
Cut the story short.

I cannot find a confidant.
I am in fire, in water.
I'll go to some corner.
Make this sword like a shield, O God.
I'll be silent; a friend; a confidant.
Tell my situation.

You made us insolent the first day.
Ask me whatever you want.
Now listen to our problems.

"I have been perturbed because
Of penniless friends," you said.
Open your lips and fill the worlds
With pearls and jewels.

"Get ready to serve with respect," you said.
If that's so, open your arms of kindness
And embrace me.

86.

Verse 2916

I have sat in fire up to my neck
Lots of times.
But today, I am in the water of union
With my Beloved, up to my neck.

I have been blessed with
All kinds of favors, up to my neck.
The Beloved was not satisfied with that.

"Are you not good for even a thorn?"
He asked while waiting for roses.
The thorn was in the ground
For nine months, up to its neck.

"What is the thorn?" I said.
"For your rose garden, like a rose,
I stayed in blood for a long time."

"You are freed from the world of struggles,
Have reached the world of love," He said.
"You were submerged, up to your neck,
In fights and troubles there."

You're free from that world,
But haven't freed yourself from you.
Your being is the shame, the fault.
You are in that shame up to your neck.

Don't set up lots of tricks
Like a pickpocket.
He is in this trap up to his neck.

The trap of this world is such a trap
That kings and lions have fallen
In its gut like dogs.
Stayed there up to their necks.

There are even more fascinating traps.
If you observe, you'll see.
The one who is out of himself is only on his hill.
But the one who has all his mind in his head
Is up to his neck.

Quit talking
You'll become short of breath.
If I wasn't tired, I would engulf you
In words up to your neck.

87.

Verse 2926

I have no fear of anyone.
Especially now that my Beloved is with me.
Why should I be afraid of even one needle?
I have Zül-fekar.[55]

How can I be thirsty?
That "river" is looking for me.
How could my heart suffer?
The One who relieves my grief is with me.

How can I be bitter?
I have been immersed in sugar.
How could winter come close to me?
My spring is next to me.

Why should I suffer fever?
Jesus is the doctor of my mind.
Why should I be afraid of the dog?
The master of the hunt is with me.

Why shouldn't I come to the assembly?
The Cupbearer is attracting me.
How can I not conquer those cities?
The Sultan is with me.

The wind in this big jar
Is fermenting, overflowing for us.
There is no place for difficulty
And lightheadedness here for us.

If I fight with fate,
Tear it to pieces,
I don't have to make excuses.
The Beautiful One is with me, next to me.

I have been immersed in wealth and blessings.
Drunk with favor and Grace
In the arms of fortune.
The Beloved, who embraces so beautifully,
Is with me.

O, the talent of orators.
O, the talent of fighters.
I am tired of words. Be silent now.
The master of conversation is by my side.

88.

Verse 2935

For a long time, the singer of the heart
Sang with love.
Then my Beloved entered from the door
With the glass in his hand.

He took all the love,
Which is like smoke in clouds,
From my head, then poured
It back into my head.
The thousand-year-old wine
Renewed our love.

The ties of sects and religions
Have killed me.
Now, I am drunk with the present moment.
I neither recognize credit of the past,
Nor future gains.

I gave the vineyard of the Soul.
I bought the barrel where grapes are crushed.
I wrote the deed of this transaction
On a glass of wine.

O clown of time,
Give up all your house of belongings.
This cup of wine has more value than that.
Once you give up everything
You will understand its value.

Close this mouth,
Open the mouth of Soul;
Then you will see.
This world is nothing but a morsel.

But when your soul becomes drunk
It doesn't even want a morsel.
Anyone who is drunk with his face,
His beauty mark,
Doesn't care for thick soup.

Souls belong to the sky.
Great souls are all
Drunks of Shems of Tebriz.
They ascend to the heights
Like drops of mist.

89.

Verse 2943

O my Beautiful, I have been
Free from you for some time; have given you up.
Still, my heart is not content.
I have been burning, melting,
At the same time, have been frozen
From you and have become ice.

Sometimes you squeeze me in your hand.
Sometimes you crush me under your feet.
Yes, you are right.
The grape won't become wine
Without being squeezed and crushed.

You reflected on Earth like sunshine.
Then slowly you took us back to that side.
You went in that direction.

You returned to the circle of Sun
Like a light through our body,
From the window of our body.

The one who sees the circle of Sun
Says, "He is alive."
The one who sees the window,
Says, "Somebody died."

He has hidden; covered
Our source, our essence,
In the glass of grief and joy.
Our origin is pure.
The rest is sediment.

O Source of the Source of heart;
O God's Shems of Tebriz,
Hundreds of hearts are roasted for you.
What's the value of
The thin layer of bread dough?

90.

Verse 2950

O Beautiful One who is pure
From water, from earth,
Step just once on my ground.
I have no hand left, no heart.
Put Your hand on my heart.

I became turbid water,
Lost in the mud.
Pick me up, pour me in Your chest.
My home will be there.

The curls of your hair
Have made my life very complicated.
Spread your hair
On my utterly disordered affairs.

Whatever I have gained,
Isn't worth anything without You.
Send the torrent of love
Over my gains.

If you want, even the Soul
Becomes a moth around my light.
Give your fire to my talented light.

I have been like a mohair garment,
Tied by hundreds of knots
Because of your hair.
But, still do me the favor
That ties me to your curly, wavey hair
For even a short time.

Beloved, the well of Babil
Is filled with spells because of your eyes.
Make a good spell. Drop me there.

You said Elest.
Since then, my Soul has been pregnant.
Make an amulet with the word "trouble."
And give it to my pregnant Soul.

When will you disperse the cloud
From your face and call me?
Put your face to mine,
Which becomes like a full moon.

O God's Shems of Tebriz,
If my Soul is happy,
Give the blessing of Union
To this happy Soul.

91.

Verse 2960

If the wind snatched the cover
From your face and flew,
Death, wherever it is,
Would come to life and move.

O One who separates
Those belongings from ours,
Stop the fight. Come to peace.
Quit anger and coyness.

O One who raises us like a happy destiny,
Gives us our wishes; one morning of joy.
You offered that big glass of Keykubad,
And we drank it.

Then mind, when it has fallen
Into the valley of separation,
Becomes drunk, passes out of itself.
If your turbid wines are like that,
How would the pure ones be?

You are our Sun.
Once you rise behind the mountain,
This cold frozen earth
Becomes warm and exuberant.

Last night you opened your lips.
Sugar and honey spread around.
You made a beautiful promise.
We started counting the days.

The drunkenness of your love
Is better than wine or opium.
Your face is brighter
Than the Sun and moon.

O Lion who catches every prey,
You wouldn't deem it proper for the heart
To burn in fire like chips and straw
By counting his faults and shame.

I am in this world
But my heart never falls into the greed
Of making the thin, half dough
Bigger or rounder with stretching.

O Love, until when will you
Be asking me why my face is so pale?
My temper is bilious.
I boil and overflow
Because of my own exuberance.
I am turning yellow, like saffron.

When will the time come
That you'll spread your black, curly hair
Over my face out of obstinancy to evil eyes?
Say, "O One who gave his heart to us,
I am giving you all."

I am neither with you,
Nor can I stand this separation.
This ruins me, destroys me.

You talk because your words remain
Like the inscriptions on stone.
Ours will be forgotten quickly.

92.

Verse 2973

O One who makes his lover
A slave and tortures him with jealousy,
All your lovers gave up the throne,
And gain with Your love.

You filtered hundreds of raindrops,
Made wine and put it in one glass.
You drank hundreds of glasses
From that wine and still stayed sober.

You threw a rope and
Pulled us to the sky.
But I stayed in the air.
The rope is broken in my hand.

So many lions have been skinned.
Their bones were broken
Because of your gazelle eyes.

What luck to see your moon face
In a dream at night.
What happiness to see
Your beauty in the morning.

O Beautiful One, even your cheapest
Slave turned into a mirror.
When the mirror was broken,
Hundreds of hands and feet were wounded.

I have glimpsed the Beauty
Of Shems of Tebriz.
Said "What a beauty. God saves
You from evil eyes."
But the arrow was already
Thrown away by jealousy.

93.

Verse 2980

Since you have been burning
With that pure, clean love now,
You will see the face
Of hundreds of houri's tomorrow.

Look at your affection, your desires.
How pure, clean, and colorless.
Look at, and see, that Earth full of beauties,
Born from that clean love.

Your Soul, which looks like a bee,
Is not seen. But look at
The honeycomb which made it.
It is full of honey.

Look at the height of your body.
Two yards, maybe even less.
But look at your Soul.
It is higher than nine skies.
Maybe even larger than that.

How long will you be licking this bowl?
Throw this jar to the ground.
Remove the cap which is made of mud
And show the top of the wine barrel.

Turn your praying rug into fire
So your prostration will be clean.
Someone with a fire-face would be born
And show his face under the praying rug.

Comes riding, the love
Of Shems of Tebriz.
The moon and sun come by foot
Behind that Sultan.

94.

Verse 2987

Someone is hidden here,
Holding my skirt.
He bent backward and grabbed
My hair, kept pulling me.

There is someone secret here,
Like Soul; better than Soul.
He has shown a garden,
Taken over my house and belongings.

Someone is hidden here
Like an image in the heart.
But the light of his face
Covers my whole Being.

Someone is secret here,
Like sugar in the sugar cane.
It is a candy man. Sweet, sweetest.
He took over my store.

Magician? Sorcerer?
Nobody sees him.
A merchant who knows all the businesses
Has taken the scale from my hands.

I am mixed with him like rose marmalade.
I took his habits.
He gained my dispositions.

I don't even see the beauties of this earth.
Only his beautiful image
Has been absorbed by my eyelashes.

I am ill. I have turned
Around the world.
Haven't found help from anyone.
At the end, I have seen his trouble.
Have taken my remedy from his hand.

You'll also find the remedy
If your heart is burned and roasted;
If you still keep turning around your troubles.

You'll bring pearls and coral
If you give up hope yourself
And plunge into the sea of desperation.

Break the spell of appearance.
Open the Soul's eye
And see my power, my splendor,
Which covers both East and West.

When you open the Soul's eye
You see the Cupbearer of Absence has come.
Greed, you kept my promise.
Offered a glass of wine.

O Noah, who knows and sees the Soul.
I hold your shirt and pull;
Because, as you see, my
Float covers the whole world.

I am asking, "Is it proper?
If you are our throne, how come
Our head is wounded?
You are our cave's friend.[56]
How come our friend
Would be a slave?"

He answered, "Quit crying.
Look at the direction from which
Your crying comes. Lovers become Soul
And obtain my sustenance."

Heartbroken friends,
Sit at the top of heart's house.
The drunks and wine worshippers
Fill all my space.

Hunt your prey like sporting dogs.
Get your wine. Don't be like
A barking dog in my barn.

You see Shemseddin of Tebriz
Has risen in the sky of Soul.
The glory of his face covers
And sparkles light on my world.

95.

Verse 3005

O my Beautiful, your love,
Just like amber, attracts the heart.
Heart has gone to you
And we, like lovers, run behind him.

The heart has stolen
A bunch of love dresses
From your beauty.
The police of Separation
Cut the hands of the heart.

My Soul eats so much sugar
At the Egypt of Love,
That sugar comes
From the reed of my wails.

O stately bird of good fortune,
Landed at the throne of God,
From the shadow of your love,
Every moment, Souls fly
To the throne, like falcons.

What a happy garden and meadow,
Where roses and iris grow
With the water of love,
And gazelles are spread all around.

The eye doesn't see itself.
But, because of your mirror,
All eyes are watching themselves
In the mirror now.

O God's Sun of Shems of Tebriz,
With your stately shrill pipe,
Tune the Rebab[57] of the Soul.
With that Soul's Rebab is His voice heard.

96.

Verse 3012

That singer came again
And started singing with the harp.
Opened the door of joy to love.

He freed the "Bazaars of Josephs" from jail;
Made the sugar stores more valuable.

He cut the heads off great men
With a sword,
But raised them up with meaning.
Gave them real greatness.

He wounded and killed lovers.
Sat in the middle of their blood,
Then got up and performed their
Namaz,[58] one by one.

I don't know who will
Have the pleasure of sharing
The curls of your hair.
We also put our necks in front
Of those curls, O my Beauty.

Eternal destiny has told you,
"I am your least important slave."
And rubbed his face at your feet.
You even showed him coyness.

For your endearment, God made
The heads of the Graceful
Bow in supplication
To the ground on which you walk.

O Jeweler of the Truth,
O God's Shems of Tebriz,
Sometimes you prune me like a vine stump.
Sometimes you make me the pruning knife.

97.
Verse 3020

Tell the intolerant bigots
It is time for repentance,
That troubled times have come.
But how can one repent
When he has such beauty, such charm?

Religious bigotry is finished.
The repentant vow not to repent again,
Because lovers have other things
To do than repent.

You escaped from the world,
Reached the light of the Soul,
Broke the foot of repentance,
When you cut your own head like a candle.

To be restless
To the gazelle of Tartar land
Is a must in love.
When Hitay's Turk comes,[59]
Repentance is a big mistake.

When He starts hunting,
He gets lots of Soul.
One arrow from his looks
Is worth hundreds of blood repentances.

His image hits, crushes the lover every dawn.
The dust which his horse breaks
Is a salve for hundreds,
A remedy for the eyes of repentance.

You repent while God's Sun,
Shems of Tebriz, is away.
But once he returns and shows his face,
Pity to repentance. Pity, pity.

98.

Verse 3027

Wake up from sleep. Jump.
Look, a brand new morning is coming,
Asking for friends; dancing
And tapping his feet.
The brand new morning is coming from the sky.

O my life, why did you sit?
It is time to drink wine, get drunk.
Nobody could get his feet loose
From this world of struggle. Fight.

Get up. For the thought of drunkenness,
The memory of a drunk, clap your hands.
Pick up the glass. Know that you have
Surpassed the chosen tent
Of the great dome of sky.

Don't look at us like ordinary drunks.
Whatever I drink, it becomes wine.
The bread I eat turns into opium
And makes my eyes dreamy.

That charmer who is the sign of resurrection,
And resurrection, itself;
The One who no eyes could see
And no ears could hear,
Doesn't let me acheive austerity.

The Fountain of Life offered me,
Free, such a wine
That one drop of it
Grew the Garden of Paradise.

Whatever I say about the Beloved,
Is all about the outside.
How does the Soul know
The secret of the inside?
How could stumpy-tailed words
Explain the secrets?

Even if His zeal
Wouldn't close my mouth,
If He let me talk,
You would see the curtains
Of hundreds of skies be torn.

What would cold, frozen soil
Know about the Sun? Know about light?
How would created Soul know Creation?

Even he doesn't know that
If he gets a small droplet,
Its drunkenness will destroy,
And pass him out of himself.

O Tebriz, how would you know
The secrets of Shemseddin?
You haven't been out
Of the hunchbacked sphere of fate.

99.

Verse 3038

O my Life, who stays in the house of heart?
Who could sit at the throne
Besides the King or Prince?

"Tell me, what do you want from me?"
The one who got drunk with wine
Pointed his hand at me and asked.
For what else would he ask
Except an appetizer and glass of wine?

An appetizer even the heart cannot reach.
A glass of wine, made by Absolute brilliance.
God is the only One who set
An eternal assembly at His solitude.

There are so many cheaters and imposters
In the gathering of wine drinkers.
They sell many deceits.
Put your mind in your head,
O soft and naive one.
Don't fall in their traps.

If you enter the circle of indifference,
If you sit with the ones who are free from care,
Don't be like a bud with its eyes closed.
Be like a rose with its mouth open.

The universe is like a mirror.
Love is the reflection of Absolute Beauty.
O people, why should the One who sees the whole
Look only at the parts?

Be on foot, like the green
At this rose garden;
Because the Beloved is the only one
Who rides a horse.
The rest of them here are on foot.

He is the sword,
Then the only one who pulls the sword.
He is the one who is killed,
Then he is the killer.
He turns into complete reasoning,
Then he is the one
Who throws reason to the wind.

That Sultan is Sellaheddin.
Pray he will be eternal,
Live a long life.
His hand of kindness and favor
Is like a necklace around my neck.

100.

Verse 3047

I have seen my Beloved
Turning around the house.
He had a stringed instrument
And kept playing a tune.

He was lost in that beautiful melody
With fiery strokes.
He was drunk with the wine of Mugh,[60]
Attracting many hearts.

He was singing the tune of Irak,[61]
Playing for the name of the cupbearer.
But his real purpose was wine.
The cupbearer was his pretext.

A beautiful cupbearer came
From somewhere, with the jar in his hand,
And put the jar between them.

First he filled the glass
With wine like fire.
Have you ever seen water burn with flame?

He picked up the glass
And offered it to that charmer
Who catches hearts,
Then prostrates and kisses the threshold.

The Beloved took the glass
And drank the wine.
The flame of this wine covered his face.

He was watching his Beauty
And telling the evil eyes,
"Nobody like me has ever come to this world,
And will never come."

101.

Verse 3055

O wise man, open the jar of wine.
Be careful so the mirror of heart
Won't be rusted and broken;
So hatred and contempt
Cannot get in between.

If you break the glass,
Lots of feet will be hurt.
In any case, this is a bad thing.

But if you put on salve,
Express your sorrow,
Caress and scratch the head of the wounded,
Thousands of them will kneel down
To the shoes of your love and kiss your feet.

Drink the wine, as much as you can.
Get better and better. Go out of
The five senses and six dimensions.
Don't leave any malice
Around the house of the heart.

But not the wine made by grapes
That grow in the ground.
Drink the wine offered by the hand of God
Without jar, without barrel.
It comes from the land of cleanliness.

If you drink this wine,
You'll find whatever you desire.
You'll get whatever you want
At the assembly of Union.
At the land of struggle and trouble.
Either this doesn't exist,
Or that can't be found.

Brand new joys come from
God's Shems of Tebriz to the Soul
Which has been plunged in grief
And trouble after trouble.
Not the old worn-out joys.

102.

Verse 3062

O charmer, whose deceits
And tricks are sweet and beautiful,
How long will You keep fooling me?
Why do You cheat the person who belongs to You?

The whole Universe is Your domain
By one good omen.
Who exists beyond Your domain?
Who are You fooling?

You deceived David with wealth and power.
In a different way, You did the same
To Job with grief and calamities.

You attract some with bait,
You lead others to the trap.
O Beautiful face, since You are
The One who deceives,
That trap becomes bait.

Pharaoh cheated the whole world,
But that villain didn't know
You were the One cheating him.

Even Your minor deceit is better
Than his hundreds of bloody ransoms.
How great is the person
Who You attract to Yourself
Without showing any valuable bait?

O Heart, if you have learned
How God persuades someone,
Then you will be able to persuade
And get everything from God.

103.

Verse 3069

If you get a smell of Soul
From that unseen, hidden Beauty,
If you find a trace, a sign from Him,
You won't be able to be contained
In hundreds of worlds.

If you see the Sun of Soul,
You become king without an army.
You'll have the land of Absence
And reach the One who knows
All the hidden secrets.

If you cannot find the treasure
You are looking for on Earth,
You will find it in the sky.

If you are not ungrateful to Love,
If you are sure,
You'll see and have
Many Chinese beauties for nothing.

You will see the Beauties
And beautiful things in Heaven
While you are still on this Earth,
In the clean, pure mirror of the heart.

If you are wounded with the arrow of Love,
If the Beloved made you drunk,
Don't worry if life goes out of your hand.
You will get hundreds of them.

If you free yourself
From the heart's anxieties,
You will find the key to the secret
Of breaking all difficult spells.
You will break them.

You break all the idols
For the sake of the Sultan of Soul
And see the sculptor who makes them.

You will obtain hundreds of interpreters
To know the signs and symbols freely
From that God's and Sheriat's[62]
Shems of Tebriz:
The one who has realized himself in God.

104.

Verse 3078

O Imam[63] of Love,
Pronounce God's greatness.
Extend your hands to the sides.
Be disgusted with your existence.
Give up your Being.

You were waiting anxiously.
It is time. Time for praying.
Get up. Jump. Don't sit.

You are worshipping hundreds of idols
Because of the love of that Beauty;
Looking in hundreds of different Kibles
To find the real Kible.

O Soul, fly high a little bit. Fly high.
O Beloved, on whose orders
Did the Soul become a slave?
Because the moon is always at the top,
Shadows are at the bottom.

Don't go to every door,
Like the poor of every house.
You are alright. Have power.
Knock at the door of the sky.

If the jar of the sky
Made you like that,
If you are out of yourself,
Be indifferent to the whole world.

I keep asking, "How do you do?
How are you?"
But who could inquire like that
To the invisible Soul?

You are very drunk tonight.
When morning comes you will see
How many glasses you have broken.
How many bags you have deflated.

Even then, I still depend on you;
Because you are the one
Who repairs all those thousands
Of broken ones.

O painter who makes secret forms
Inside of our Soul,
You have hundreds of thousands
Of paintings besides the moon and sun.

If you close one door,
You open a hundred doors.
If you break one heart,
You'll give hundreds of hearts
Hundreds of Souls.

I become crazy, insane.
Whatever I say, I say from my craziness.
If you are the confidant of Elest,
You say, "Yes, yes," to my crazy words.

105.

Verse 3090

O one who makes a face
Like he's been drinking vinegar,
What would happen if you smiled once?
I swear to God, you haven't
Changed from this sour-faced one at all.

Take the bitterness, give sugar.
Give your life. You are a nice person.
Have a high opinion of yourself.
At least die with a smile.

The moon has become thin, like hair,
Still, it keeps laughing.
What would happen if
You also become like that?

Flowers grow and bloom in the wetland.
You are an unripe grape.
Don't you have a Soul?
How long will you live, being needy?

How can a rat rise to the heights
From the rathole?
You settled down at the mine of troubles.
What can you see from there?

They will find the Archangel Gabriel
Above the dome of the sky.
They find safety and security on the ground,
Where the clean, harmless people walk.

Your face, the color of your face
Tells where you are from,
Who your friends are, what your secret is.

It is obvious to the one who can see,
Whether you are wise and intelligent
Or someone who has just opened his eyes.

Karun[64] went down the well
Like a bucket.
Jesus ascended the dome of the sky
With the rope he threw to the sky.

Even if it ascends,
The bucket would only carry well water.
Rot and decay are at the bottom of the well.

O Graceful ones, fly above, to the heights.
Free yourselves from specters;
From the bounds of "how" and "what."
Fly to the heights.

106.

Verse 3101

O smiling spring, bring us something
From the land of Absence.
Tell us about our Beloved.

You are smiling. Your face is clean, fresh.
You are full of green and smell like musk.
You either have the same color as our Beloved,
Or you took this color from Him.

O season, You are nice,
Like soul hidden from eyes.
You manifest with your signs,
But you are concealed.

O Rose, why don't you smile?
Your separation is ended.
O cloud, why don't you cry?
You are separated from your Beloved.

O Rose adorning the green, smile openly,
Because you kept hiding
Inside the thorns
For the last three months.

O Garden, feed and grow
These newcomers well.
Because you heard from thunder
How they came.

O Wind, move the branches.
Someday you will blow them
To the time of Union.
Remember that. Move the branches.

Look at the trees. Cheerful like lucky people.
O Violet, why is your neck bent with sorrow?

The Iris said to the bud,
"Your eyes are closed, but day by day
You are reaching a happy destiny.
Congratulations. You are lucky."

107.

Verse 3110

O One who made rose marmalade
Out of our Soul,
You took the Soul and heart,
Then You left us.

You have seen us fall to the ground
Without feet, like a shadow.
Like a cypress which grows from the top.
O Beloved, You gave up the shadow.

We are running this way and that,
Like the torrents in the forest,
To the top of the mountain, after you.
You, like the fountain of spring,
Are running in a different direction.

You are such a moon.
Catching the one who comes to Your harvest
And pulling to the gold's mine like the sun.

You kill us with jealousy.
Since You have an eye on us,
Keep us, like tears in Your eyes.
Don't drop us out of Your eyes.

Your lover has been hurt
On a hundred sides.
People keep blaming him in every way.
But You are shielding him
With Your mercy and kindness.

You tricked some people.
Tied them up with gold chains.
The others, with proof and evidence,
You threw to hell.

Alas, one bad person
Has hurt several naive people.
But You pity the one whom
You lead into evil things.

Your lovers' sleep is all gone.
Their eyes are open all night long,
Because You pulled them to Yourself at dawn.

O Love, You don't have
A heart to burn, to ruin,
Even though You are
The One who attracts all hearts.

Enough. Be silent now.
You are not by yourself. You are drunk.
You took the snack which was to serve Jesus
To the stable and put it in front of the donkey.

108.

Verse 3121

If you make a nest
For a bird in the pigeon loft,
It doesn't matter how big or long it is,
A camel can't fit there.

That pigeon loft is the mind.
That nest is your body.
The camel, with his height, is Love—
The beauty of Love.

That bird cannot drink
From the big jar of the Sultan.
Even if you open hundreds of narrows
Or open closed boxes,
You cannot get the smell.

Beloved, don't look for
The secret of that truth from us.
I have been involved and overwhelmed
By temporary witticisms.

I have seen a paper
Written at great length.
I hung it on my neck
Like an amulet, as a joke.

But that divine amulet
Became heavier and heavier.
Reached the point that
A thousand Arab horses couldn't carry it.

While I tore the curtains
With the flame that comes from Hicaz,[65]
My own curtains have been torn.

It is time to love,
God's Shems of Tebriz.
When His love roars and overflows,
It will tear all the curtains.

109.

Verse 3129

Since you are in the casino,
You'll surely gamble.
Since you started this business,
Even if it is temporary,
At the end you will reach the truth.

O my dear friend,
Be kind. Get along with everyone.
This is the place to make a profit.
Why don't you take the opportunity
To make a big profit?

You say I am busy praying, day and night.
But, O my brother,
Your words don't belong in prayers.

Don't get involved with unsavory ones.
If your head is high,
If you are great,
Be involved with Kings.

You put on human clothes.
You have the most beautiful,
The most distinguished, shape.
Since things are like that,
Why do you keep getting black
Like a frying pan?

O one who hangs around with Sultans,
Since so many Arab horses, under your order,
Are waiting for you,
Why do you ride this donkey?

Hit this glass heart
To the stone of the Beloved.
Come to His assembly and
See how to please
And take care of the heart.

The Sultan will blow such
A breath to your heart
That you'll be free from music,
From the mode of Hicaz.

You tap your feet on the ground like a drunk
And enter the assembly
Of the moon-faced Beauty.
You keep looking at the face
Of that Beauty and sway like a Sultan.

The Sultan compliments you, saying
"O purest of the pure, guide the close ones.
Always be at our temple,
Because you are the confidant
Of the secrets of the trusted one."

Sometimes, you admire his Beauty.
Sometimes, you drink wine, become drunk.
Sometimes, you give yourself to him, get closer.
Sometimes, you are coy with him.

I mean Shemseddin when I say,
"Throne, our master, our owner."
I am like two different, unrelated people
At his temple. Where is he? Where am I?

Whoever has air from Tebriz,
Even if he is Indian,
Will become a rose-faced Turk.

110.

Verse 3142

If that moon-faced one rose in your heart
Would you be able to recognize him?
How does He come to the Heart?
Unexpectedly, and not the customary way.

If you say, "I will recognize Him,"
This is a very important word. A big matter.
If you say, "How would I know?
This is a denial, almost a blasphemy.

In fact, people keep busy, turning around
With the dilemma of "I know, I don't know."
They are like a camel.
When its eyes are covered, it keeps turning around.

Keep turning in silence, involuntarily.
Don't even try to raise your head or complain.
You are tied. Your ropes are in His hand.

A blind man bought Joseph
With eighteen counterfeit coins.
Because the owner was greedy,
The seller was blind.

You are like Joseph,
Fallen into the well of the flesh.
Here is the rope. Climb outside.
Free yourself from the grief
And frustration of the Earth.

O Nefs-i Mutmainne,[66]
Cover yourself with God's attributes.
Here are the heavy dresses.
How long will you wear that torn, old mantle?

The moon comes out of eclipse
When metal cups bang against each other.[67]
I am the One who covers your moon.
Give me a sound. The moon will be free
And shine again.

Adam ate a grain from the wheat,
Which will eventually be harvested.
But You are the Hyacinth of Union,
You are sure You won't be cut with a sickle.

If I don't tell a gazel,
He splits my mouth and says,
"Play. Sing. Increase the words, the joy.
After all, you are the drummer," he says.

111.

Verse 3152

We don't hold a shield
In front of our face in the war.
When we do Sema,[68] we are aware
Of neither the reed nor tambourine.

We have been annihilated with His love.
Spread under the feet of love.
We are layer upon layer of love.
Not bald or deaf.

We have struggled with ourselves.
Annihilated our existence.
Become the absolute lover.
We don't have anything but Nazar.[69]
What will salve do for us?

The body that is nothing but attributes,
Becomes Soul and heart for malice
And will burn to ashes, melt all sicknesses.
The worst disease is to be frozen.

From the intensity of that fire and melting,
From the love of that favor,
My lungs have turned into blood.
I don't have lungs anymore.

My heart has been broken
Into a hundred pieces.
Has become a vagabond.
If you look for a heart in me today,
You won't see a trace of it.

If you look at the circle
Of the moon in the sky,
It becomes smaller every day.
At the end, it disappears entirely.

The moon's disappearance from the sky
Is the result of the sun.
It comes back later,
But it is not the same.

My Sultan, send the planet Venus
To the land of heart to play and sing;
Because the reed and tambourine are not suitable
At the Sema gathering of Souls.

No. No, in the place where even the sun
Feels incapable of what Venus can do,
Not every player or instrument
Would be able to stand the temperature.

112.

Verse 3162

You came to confuse;
To ruin us with excitement.
You are the present-day David
With the melody of that Zebur.[70]

You are either Egypt, full of sugar cane,
Or the beauty of Joseph, full of life.
Why don't you ask Jacob
If he could stand that suffering
With this patience?

That tumult came again
With instigations and blame.
"You are either the Sun," I said,
"Or the glory of Glory."

O sky, you keep turning with indecision.
O Earth, you keep silent with sorrow.
Stay calm, in repose.

O Charmer, who is more beautiful than fairies;
O Charmer, who has such sweet instigation,
Heart doesn't want to tell his name
Because he is so jealous.

After the sun rises, I wonder
Why it shows its face
So blindly and ignorantly,
Since your face is so much brighter.

Why have you stayed behind the curtain?
Why haven't you been disgraced publicly?
This is not from obstinacy.
This is from stupidity.

That falcon came again:
The one who hunts cryers and beggars.
If you are not an owl of ill omen,
Not sinister, why are you
Flying away from Him?

The one who knows doesn't care for this idea.
You took this and put it in your head.
Pay attention and see how far
You are from Him. How far?

He became manifest
From the Greatest of the Great temple.
O Soul, yell and scream.
You are the Mount Sinai of Moses.

O Kible of our time,
Come home again.
I swear to God that you
Are the Salâh of religion[71]
And keep appearing all the time.

113.

Verse 3174

With thousands of tales and deceits,
The image of such a friend comes,
That wherever there is such a beauty,
He would die in front of His feet.

You have seen many beauties.
You have heard charmers like the houris.
But come here and look
At the Beloved. See His charm.

When my Soul found Him,
My being disappeared.
When I touched His feet,
I lost my hand. Can't do anything now.

O player, my God,
For the sake of the Sultan
Play that tune with the harp.

There is new, unseen excitement in the heart
From those beautiful faces.
My pale face will turn
Into pure gold because of Him.

They asked me, "Why are you crying
In these two worlds? What is this wail?"
I told them, "Yes. That wail is
Enough for me in two worlds."

I have seen the Sultan while hunting.
That moon was filled with joy, laughing,
Riding his horse in the dust.

He threw an arrow with his eyes.
A big, hard arrow.
He threw to such a lean prey.

A thorn has pierced my heart
From the rose garden of His love.
A thorn, but such a thorn,
That hundreds of rose gardens
Would be slave and servant for it.

What is Soul for the pleasure
Of your love? A piece of dust.
What is Soul for the light of your sun?
Only a drop of mist.

God should be your enemy
If you talk about roses
Or mention the Plain tree in
The Love garden of your face.

We became poets because of
Your magic eyes.
We cannot fall in love with someone else.
We have a big excuse.

Will I be able to see a day
That the Sultan comes swaying;
Sending glory to the whole of existence
From His fiery face?

Will I be able to see
My bitter soul sweetened by His honey?
Will I be able to see a new excitement
Fall on my Soul with His spark?

Tebriz of love, now become
A song for every ear, an excursion
For every eye with
The love of Shemseddin.

114.

Verse 3189

I have complaints for you.
Why are you like that, Beloved?
I am sick. I feel weak.
Why don't you come and see me?

You have seen me so pale
You thought I had died.
How could anybody
Who has been your friend die?

You haven't even bothered
To ask how I was doing while
I was burning with fever.
O my Master, my Soul,
You haven't even heard my moaning.
O, my health, my cure.

I hesitated. I waited patiently
For a long time.
But today, I started showing coyness
To the source of coyness and gracefulness.

The medicine of my Soul
Comes when the moon rises tonight.
Then, O troubles and griefs,
You will turn into wax
Even though you are towers of iron.

Night inquires about this poor one's health
Regardless of how late the time is.
And, without that big jar, without anything
To eat, would become drunk and leave.

O wail, how long will you last?
You are more than morning dew.
You also set a trap for that poor, worthless man.

115.

Verse 3196

O Brother, what would happen
If you didn't sleep one night?
If you stayed awake like a candle, a spark?

The doors of the sky are open at night.
Fortune is open at night.
If you stay awake like the moon,
Your star will shine, become beautiful.

If you belong to the sky
You always desire that world.
You don't stay anywhere but the sky.
Don't sleep anywhere but the heights.

When Abyssinian soldiers
Attack the land of Rum,
Don't sleep. Defend the land like Caesar.

Your are the Jesus of time.
Journey at night, walk straight, circle.
Don't sleep in the mud like a donkey, O Soul.

Good times are made at night.
Stages are reached at night.
If you want the Sultan,
Don't sleep on the journey.

Lucky, auspicious people
Are in the shadow of God.
Don't ever sleep anywhere else, brother.

Didn't Joseph get in trouble
When he left his father?
You are also Joseph.
Be careful. If you sleep,
Sleep with your father.

Your brother plotted against you.
Put your mind into your head.
Be aware if you sleep among them.

Shems of Tebriz, keep going
On the road.
You are also on a journey.
Don't sleep on the road.

116.

Verse 3206

Beloved, don't cover your
Flaming, shining face for one moment.
I will be overjoyed, will overflow.
Then you ask me "How long
Will you be boiling, overflowing?"

When you set the rule
Of wine drinking like that,
How can that poor Soul,
That poor mind, be calmed,
After being so exuberant?

You are the one who keeps
Blowing the reed of Soul every moment.
If you are in ecstasy and rapture,
Why do you blame the reed?

Brilliance like that cannot be covered.
If hundreds of veils cover your face,
It still cannot be hidden.

O naive, inexperienced love,
You are fooled by appearance.
Keep turning around the blaze.
You are either a bloody murderer
Or a dazzling jackal.

If you were wise,
How did you become insane?
If you don't belong to love,
Why did you get involved with love?

I have seen all my particles
In silence at that temple.
But under every silence
I heard shouting.

I asked Shems of Tebriz,
"Who are these silent ones?"
He said, "When the time comes,
You'll learn all about them."

117.

Verse 3214

He spread a cover in the fire.
Be like that, my Beloved.
Then he was hidden inside the fire.
Be like that, my Beloved.

The cover became so beautiful.
My candle has burned with so much desire,
Cried, shed so many tears, and melted.
Be like that, my Beloved.

Since we came back to love,
We cannot sleep at night.
Be like that at the gathering
Of the drunks, my Beloved.

Lovers are all up.
They can't sleep at night.
Don't leave the gathering. Don't run away.
Be like that, my Beloved.

Union runs like a torrent.
Mecnun becomes Leyla.[72]
Now is night, tomorrow will be day.
But with all this,
Be like that, my Beloved.

God has become manifest,
Showed kindness and favor to the speaker.
I saw a fire in reality.
Be like that, my Beloved.

118.

Verse 3220

You are smelling like roast.
Your heart has burned, is fried.
Come back to your senses.
Find whatever you have lost.

If you act too big in this world,
Your head will be bowed in the real one.
But if you make yourself a slave to Him,
I will become a slave to you.

My Hodja,[73] never mind this road.
Tell us about the Sultan.
If you are drunk with that wine,
Open your mouth. Let me smell your breath.

Yesterday, the charmer offered
A golden cup and said,
"If you are half sleepy-drunk,
Drink one more glass."

"I cannot get up," I said.
He insisted. "Even if you fall
On the ground, I will pour
This glass on your head."

Really, he poured the glass on my head.
I saw the Earth completely disappear;
Turn into a rough sea with big waves.
I was like a seagull there.

Hodja, don't get mad, be calm.
Don't keep shaking your head.
It is not our fault if you don't understand.

I told the secret of God,
But I told it at the bottom of the well.
You are intimate to the curtain and veil,
That is why I said, "The moon is black."

O God's Sun of Tebriz,
I closed my mouth; will keep silent now
Because you are such a sun, that not
Every eye could stand your light.

119.

Verse 3229

"I want to go hunting," you said.
You have gone, become hunted.
They hunt you.
"I will find peace," you said.
You have become totally restless, without peace.

How can I not call you Hizir?
You drank from the Fountain of Life.
How can I not die in front of you?
You have become Beloved to the Beloved.

How can I not turn around you?
You are the house of God.
How can I not kiss your feet?
You drag your feet,
And have reached eternity.

How can I not drink your cup?
You are the cupbearer to Being.
How can I not eat your snack?
You keep spreading sugar.

How can you not be Fâruk?[74]
You are saved from separation.
How can you not be Siddiyk?
You have become a friend
To the friends of the cave.

Since you've become a slave to Him,
You are a sultan now.
Since you've become weak and tired with grief,
You have grown and become stronger now.

You have seen His rose garden;
Gathered hundred of different roses.
At the same time, you touched
His hyacinth and returned to the tulip garden.

Did you see his eyes, God?
We trust in God from those eyes,
Which stage a hold-up, even in sleep.
Those eyes half-closed, half-sleepy from wine.

You stole so many mantles
When you were poor.
Alas for the poor.
Now you've become the Zul-fekaar.[75]

Get up. Pull up and throw away
The dead roots.
Because you are the sound of Gabriel's trumpet,
Cut the neck of the fallen.
You are the springs.

You are saved from Judgment Day
Because You are the last day of time.
You are free from counting
Because you cannot be contained by numbers.

You don't need bread
Like the fish in the sea.
You don't care for water either.
You turn into a lizard.

O pure Soul, the one kneaded with God's glory,
You are free from choices and willpower.
Look at this.
You've become willpower and choice.

You stayed away from the desires of Self.
Gave up your wishes in two or three days.
Now, you want everyone to reach their desires
Because you have already reached yours.

You were a game for grief
Before you had a helper.
Now, you have all the power
And have reached God,
Who is absolute power
And manages everything.

If you shed the people's blood,
Fight with destiny,
You don't need any excuses.
You become a rose-cheeked Beauty.

Your coyness is tolerated
Because you are beautiful and charming.
If you act great, it is alright,
Because you belong to the great ones.

You turned out to be earrings to the ears.
But still, to say something meaningful,
Get in the circle of silent ones
And be silent.

120.

Verse 3247

You made an oath, repented yesterday.
Today, you broke both.
Yesterday, you were a bitter sea.
Today, you become a pearl.

Yesterday, you were Beyazid,[76]
Adding Being to your Being.
Today, you fall on the ground,
Selling wine with sediment;
And you are drunk.

Drink that sedimented wine, O Soul.
Quit. Give up the mind, O Soul.
While worshipping idols, don't dress in green.
Don't try to appear Sufi, O Soul.

Today, you are a river,
At the same time, a glass
Filled by the sun.
You are neither a bridegroom
Of a moon-faced beauty,
Nor the husband of the moon.

You can't fit in with a house and family.
You are beyond meaning.
You don't resemble anyone.
You are as you are.

There was a corner. That corner was closed.
You were worried and unhappy about it.
Now, you opened that closed place
And freed yourself.

Animals don't ride, they are
Usually ridden for work.
You are not an animal.
You are higher than that.
You are saved from being ridden to work.

You are the messenger in the sky.
When will you ride like the moon
With the news arrow in your hand?
Send this to the world.

Be silent. Don't show any sign or trace,
Although every word of yours
Is like medicine for those whose heart is hurt.
Still, be silent.

121.

Verse 3256

Even though you wear course woolen stuff,
You are Keykubad.
Even though you are hidden from eyes,
You are the fire in the Soul,
The remembrance in the heart.

You entered as a form,
Dressed with shape.
But You are in the sky.
You are the pole for
The nine-level sky;
The lamp in it.

You have tied our Being
To the land of Absolute Absence.
To attain our desire,
You gave us failure and frustration.

You did this because You wanted
Only the lion and lion cub
To reach your temple.
Not the one whose legs are shakey.

You wished that man would
Leave his head before he enters Your temple,
And hear the voice of "O my creature,"
Without the use of his ears.

You get one month's road
In one day, because you are
Riding the horse of the wind, like Solomon.

What is gold?
What is silver?
Bring the storehouse of Soul
And give Soul if you are generous.
Never mind money and wealth.

O my Beauty, for your way
There is no need for a guide.
Because on this road,
The one who goes and the one who guides
Are halo and moonlight.

The moon carries its light
From place to place
Like the Arab drags
His camel from stage to stage.

A large bouquet will come
From the sweet basil
Which grows from the trouble
You go through—the beliefs you have.

Don't blame Solomon
Because you were lost.
It doesn't matter.
The Hoopoe bird is looking for you.
That's enough for you.

O my friend, this is just
The beginning of salvation;
Reaching your wishes.
Daylight broke. Wake up from sleep.

The Sun is shining without cover or curtain.
Victory and help keep coming
Without even trying.

The Soul is dipped into wine.
The glass keeps turning.
Grief and sorrow were chased away.
Thanks are getting longer.

122.

Verse 3270

There is an Aloe wood
In the land of Absence, burning.
This Love is its smoke.
There is an existence
Painted with non-existence,
From which comes every Being.

A Being is free from any defect, any fault.
Put a curtain at the Land of Absence.
That Absence is like a fire
Behind this curtain.

Smoke, although it is born from fire,
Still covers the fire.
Pass through the smoke of existence.
There is nothing in that smoke.

If the Soul passes through the smoke,
It will be Glory itself.
Soul is like a candle;
Body is the dish in which it stands.
Soul is like water;
Body is the riverbed.

Soul will go up when man falls down;
Even break the circle of fate.
If Soul grabs Absence, he will be better
Than existence, reaching to Absolute Being.

Soul will prepare the Universe for you,
From the Pleiades to the throne of God;
Will pick up the pearl of eternity
From the bottom of the seven oceans.

He will give up wet or dry gladly, happily.
Will go to that side.
Become confident of Love and reach Beauty.

If Shems of Tebriz accepted
Him as a confidant,
He would see Absence with the eye
Of certainty, and appear in that world.

123.

Verse 3278

Either I became funny
Or you did. You drank
Of all those glasses.
Didn't offer me one.

You are drunk with wine.
I am drunk with hope and wishes.
There is no lack of hope and wishes
At the assembly of such a Keykubad.

You killed so many lovers.
But still you are innocent
Because you didn't kill them
With pain or brutality.
You killed them with joy and pleasures.

The world opens and enlightens with You.
Humans reach their attainment and desire with You.
If things are like that, O my Beauty,
Why have you made the village
Of hopelessness your home?

Yes, I know why.
Because a bright light appears
In the darkness of night.
Cure come to the troubled one.
That is the important point.

In order to drink nothing but your grief,
Neither tell the subtle point of Amid,[77]
Or hear the words of Imad.[78]
You hold my mouth, my ear.

Carry greetings to Shems of Tebriz
From drunks. And after
You prostrate yourself to him,
Ask "Did you run away to Solitude,
O my life, my Soul?"

124.

Verse 3285

If you are dizzy with last night's wine,
And if you are still half drunk,
Don't touch our glass.
You have nothing to do with that.

If your drunkenness is gone,
Come. Sit and drink this glass.
Don't scratch your head
By falling into the reflections of the past.

You'll have no interest with others
If you worship stone.
You don't deserve the sea
As long as you remember the creek.

Those people who strive and scheme
Are not tolerated at the King's temple.
Every poor one's basket
Is extended to the Sultan.

Where are they,
The generosities of the Badya?[79]
It is impossible to be in heaven
And at the same time in
The flames of the fire.

If you see a single thread
Of that Chinese beauty's hair,
Neither the notes nor wails
Of the Zir[80] tunes will remain.

You neither boil unripened grapes,
Nor sell the vinegar.
You only drink wine and squeeze grapes.

To squeeze this grape
Of existence is good for you.
Assume: If you didn't have any existence,
To whom would it be of interest?

If you escape to the side
Of Shems of Tebriz,
God knows what kind
Of tulip garden you have entered.

125.

Verse 3294

My friend, either you are
Dark or bright-hearted.
Don't give up the Beloved.
Don't become separated from Him.

In both cases,
To draw back from him is blasphemy.
For lovers, to run away from the Beloved
Is a hundred times more
Blasphemous than blasphemy.

Your cleanness becomes dirty
When you give up Beauty.
But if you plunge into the fountain,
Even your dirt will be cleansed.

If you grabbed the tail of a lion,
You would always have roast meat.
If you are a friend of a rich man,
How can you be hungry?

Give up malice.
You have been hiding.
Don't cover yourself.
In wisdom, in understanding,
You are like a hair that
Appears inside of the glass of milk.

For poison, "What would God miss
From that?" you asked.
It is true. God is disdainful of that.
You'll die from poison.

Even if you are tired, lazy,
Or very old, try to go
Under the date tree, like Mary.

Under the shade of the date tree
You'll be sweetened like a date.
Mature from the maturity of the date tree.

126.

Verse 3302

I turned into earth
So you would spread pearls on me.
I became very thin, like hair,
So you could scratch my head.

In order for you to hold my hand,
I am washed away from my Being.
I turned into a specter
So you would come into my heart.

I have been in love day and night,
So you would rise like a moon
From the East of my heart.
I tear my collar with love.

I thought the springs of your Beauty
Would turn me into a spring.
I shed tears like spring's cloud.

I put around my neck and carry
The Trust,[81] which skies couldn't carry,
With the help of your grace.

You change every moment
To a new shape and form
For the plate of Heart.

Do a favor please.
Show a shape and form that
Cannot fit in the heart,
So idol worshippers will quit worshipping
And idol makers will quit making idols.

127.

Verse 3309

O Beloved, what a beautiful time.
Listen, for the sake of friendship.
Listen, for the sake of Love.
Mercy to the wishes of my heart.
Don't try to hurt and trouble me.

Don't treat my heart with contempt.
Don't be withdrawn from our side.
See, watch, know our situation.
Don't go away. Don't make our life bitter.

You are the real cupbearer of Soul.
Give us the morning's wine.
Night turned its face away
And is gone. The full moon is hidden.

O one who took our mind and thought,
Remember what shape we were in last night.
You offered cup after cup to us.
We are still drunk.

You ruined us, drowned us with wine.
In the end, all our secrets
Came out and spread around.

You are our Sultan
The Leyla of our nights,
The beauty of our days.

O secret of Mount Sinai,
O light of the seeing eyes,
You are great among us.
Mercy to the small ones.

Now a bout of craziness comes.
Our drunkenness is increased,
O Beautiful one who intoxicates the mind,
Who destroys shame and dignity.

Sultans of words came.
The wave of the words overflows.
But we are only voices.
The one who recites the most
Auspicious things says
The most beautiful words are God.

128.

Verse 3318

It was ordered for us.
Pleasure, peace, weddings,
They are all for us.
They were given for us to increase
The pleasures of the Moslem,
Blind the eyes of the heretic.

Every day, our new sermon is read.
Every night is a new wedding night for us.
Every moment, a handful of pearls
Are spread on us.

Love is more beautiful than it appears.
Absence is sounder than it stands.
If you kiss the hands of both,
You step to the sky.

Soul is a light
Hidden under the basin of body.
Even the sun obeys his light;
Fawns on him.

He has hundreds of different possessions and wealth.
Has hundreds of thrones and destinies.
His throne is made of greatness;
Not like the night's,
Which is made of black ebony wood.

His wealth and possessions are made
Of the light of Glory,
Protected in the chest of God;
Neither is carried on the groom's horse,
Nor has moth holes eaten in it.

I became a fire worshipper because
Of the pleasure of the Heart's fire;
And am burning with fire.
But not like Zorastrian's
Involvement with fire.

The poor Soul became a friend
With the flesh for a few days.
But, like Merguzle with Rey'li,
Or like Magribli with Tuslu,[82]
They never knew or understood each other.

The earth is like a sieve.
We are the flour in it.
Once we go through the sieve
We are pure.
Before that, we are straw.

Every day in the bazaar
Of these ordinary people,
Such things are heard:
"O poor immature man, come here.
Our material is good.
Our garment won't wear out."

Break the mold of the jar.
Pick up the cup that is filled to the rim.
How long will you be licking the bowl?
How long will you be fawning?

Will you allow me to tell the end of this:
That the destiny which has no bad omen,
No bad luck, covers East and West?

129.

Verse 3330

Since you are drunk with wine,
Hit yourself on a stone like a bottle.
Let it be broken.
You'll have a bad name for the love of Soul,
But you'll have a good reputation.

If you sit, sit like a carafe full of pleasure.
If you get up, raise up like a glass
To give joy to the people.

Your mind is a tie to your feet.
Your love is greatness.
Mind is in the land of reproach.
Love is to drink ecstasy.

The rooster, every morning, announces
The end of night.
Morning appears from the heart of darkness.

There is no Beloved but ourselves.
No wine, but our blood.
Soul is the master and slave
At the same time.

O Soul, you burned the heart,
Turned blood into wine.
O the leader of creatures,
The greatest of men!

If you want to drink this vintage wine,
Get down from the horse of thought.
Be on foot.

Müstef'ilün, faülün. Don't get excited.
Calm down, because it is time
To mature. Don't be vain.

The wine blows like the wind.
Grief escapes like a fly.
Don't forget drunks. Take care of them.

Say what You wish.
Your order is our command.
You are the Sultan, greetings to You.
You have our submission.
We are under Your order.

Tebriz should cheer because
Of the shining of Shemseddin.
Because when the Sun rises and walks,
It will enlighten everywhere
And protect both East and West.

130.

Verse 3341

O Soul, forget having
A good name and reputation.
Take it out of your heart completely.
Then you will learn all
The secrets, one by one.

O God's lover, you worry
About people's blame.
You are concerned with shame and dignity.
In the world of love, it is immature
To be bound with shame or dignity
Or to act like a Sultan.

A lover should be sweet
Beyond the bonds of why and how.
He should have great soul,
Because that temple is very high.

All this existence is like
A sty growing on Soul's eye.
Throw this robe if you are in love.
In love, those hairs are dark like evening.

Knowledge is ignorance
In the land of love.
Knowledge is not honorable there.
The uneducated lover is much greater
Than the scholar of everyday sciences.

Love came from an unseen traceless side.
The side of different knowledge, or ignorance;
From the place where
Your Soul gets the Soul of Souls.

I saw Him as a full moon
Above the roof without a house.
I admired His grace so much,
I got stuck at the door.

Either I became drunk,
Or I became wine.
I am not the drunk of reed nor tambourine.
I drank His grace,
That made me drunk.

There is a face like fire,
Covered with hair,
Which attracts heart.
Soul is trapped in the curls of that hair
And becomes a slave with its own desire.

Your grief says, angrily,
"It is time to shed your blood."
O heart; O Soul,
Who are you in front of Him?

O Soul, you surrendered to Him
On the night you were born.
You gave whatever He asked.
You submitted yourself.

O Soul, you flew to a coast.
You stayed, grew there.
You gave your heart, but you earned Beauty.
You became a slave, a servant.

O Shems, the Sun of every person
Whose mind is diverted or gone,
O rule and order of Tebriz,
Be either unconventional or mean.
You are our companion. You are our peer.

131.

Verse 3354

Once you pull the string
Of the bow of supplication,
Once you strike the plectrum of desire,
The lazy ones in the street
Become busy, hard workers.

O love, when you come
With that beauty and charm,
You pull the skirt of the soul
And take him to the Beloved.

You give such security to the soul
Out of contrariness to
The blind ones on the road.
You are hanging on the gallows
Those who steal heart.

You offer a relaxing medicine
For lovers of the Soul.
You make them cry, and pull those
Whose faces become pale
With the color of gold
Because of their love for gold.

You show the rose garden
To the one who is separated
From the Beloved, pulling thorns.
But you are sending those with
Faces like roses, and tempers
Like thorns, toward thorns.

You send Moses, who walks on ground,
To the sea.
Drive the Pharaoh, who wants to be great,
To malice and embarrassment.

Moses had a staff for help and company.
You turned this into a snake.
He carries it like a snake.

When Moses touched the snake,
He found his staff.
You did that upside down,
The way a horseshoe is nailed.

You'll find a way to dip in water
The one who falls into fire.
You send to the fire
The one who dives in water.

He drank wine, open-hearted, drunk.
How beautiful, O heart.
You'll bring him out in the open
By pulling him by his turban
From behind the curtain.

Don't give us to someone else.
He would pull us toward himself.
You pull us. Your attraction
Is so beautiful, so royal.

When a friend is well and alive,
You block his way with a mountain.
When You kill him with grief,
You take him to the cave
And become his friend.

Be silent. Drink the secret with silence.
Because when you are silent,
You look like you are smoking hashish.

132.

Verse 3367

Tremble, O gold leaves, silver birdsongs.
You are the essence of essence.
Be sure of what you look for.
It is you. It is in you.

The Sun rises, wants Particles to dance.
You may as well, O Particle.
Keep dancing. Keep whirling your skirt.

There will be a day, O Particle,
When the sun will embarrass you
And take you in his arms.
Do you know this subtle point?

He'll offer you wine and say,
"O Particle, drink this."
When you drink, you'll be annihilated.
You'll reach nothingness
In the Sun of the Soul's existence.

With the Glory of Manifestation,
Particle becomes Sun without reproach of
"You won't be able to see me."[83]

We are unripened fruits.
We will keep dancing under
The heat and light of the Sun.
Because you are the mature One, ripen us.

Bravo, O mature One.
Applause to you, O maturation;
O apprentice of the Sun of the Soul,
The One whose trace
And sign unseen are not apparent.

O Soul, O heart, as you know,
All Souls have surrendered to you.
My Shemseddin, whom everybody serves,
You are the Sultan of Sultans
Grown in Tebriz.

133.

Verse 3375

O pearl of God, mirror of meaning,
With the light of your face,
You are a gift to the throne of God.

Even the throne asked God,
"From where is that light coming,
Which reflects on me?"
God felt jealous and said to the throne,
"You don't know this."

Throne was surprised at God's jealousy.
Because "You will never be able to see me."
That news also comes from his jealousy.

If one sparkles from this light,
Reflects to the sky,
Hundreds of moons will
Appear in the sky.

Eternal kindness would be
Seen on every moon.
Every lover would see the love
Of his heart's desire.

It won't be the trouble of desire
On the route of the people's journey.
It won't be fear of nothingness
On the earth.

You breathed into it once and
Life came to a skeleton.[84]
Breathe once more for Soul
To come forth.

One spark of Your face
Changed the land of nothingness
To the land of existence.
Your lightning will reverse this
Back to the land of nothingness.

If You put Your ruby ring
In front as a charm,
All the ruby mines will scream and yell.

You offer one glass.
Everything we have has gone to the pawnshop.
Offer one more to find
The remedy for that, as You know.

A kind of Soul came to us
From God's Shems of Tebriz,
That keeps pleasing all the souls
In the land of nothingness.

134.

Verse 3386

O one who has a sign
Of his existence on both worlds,
You know well. You wounded
This sign so much.

Wound once more. I don't
Want salve from you.
It is not grief if the
Whole universe disappears.
You are hundreds of universes.

It is impossible to describe you.
You are the explanation of God's secret.
You are the Soul of Soul.
Why don't you come to the Soul?

Your art of influence is like
A wind which blows here and returns.
We are like trees. The wind is unseen;
Hidden, but knows what to do.

Because of this wind,
We become green, yellow.
But if you drop the leaves,
How can you grow fruit?

In appearance, the garden comes first;
But in truth, fruit comes first,
Because the purpose of the garden is fruit.[85]
You show the first pearl at the end.

I want to talk about you all the time,
Only to tell you to forget everyone else.
But you always hide and put us in line.

135.

Verse 3393

O the shame of living.
Look at the face of the pure Beloved,
So the color of life
Will come to your face.

Every particle is running to find life.
Don't you have a desire for life?
Not even a particle?

If life was a stone, for instance,
Springs would still come.
Rivers would flow from that living stone.

I have seen a passing image
In the mirror. I asked, "What is that?"
He answered, "I am the dust of life."

You will find real life
In the world of Eternity.
Who are they?
They are the ones who suffer
During their lives.

The ones who love peace, escape;
Give up life.
The no-good ones are the ones
Who stay in the struggle of life.

136.

Verse 3399

This Soul was hurt, bruised.
That new, better one has appeared.
This world has gone down.
That new, different one came forward.

The mine is full of holes;
With the wound of pickaxes.
But look at the goldsmith's store.
There, there is gold everywhere.

Thought doesn't come to your mind
Until you become quiet.
When Heart opens his mouth,
This mouth will be closed.

Thousands of houses fill the earth.
Thousands of buildings secretly existed
In the mind of the architect
Before coming to this world.

There is another secret:
That all which comes to the mind
Of the architect, or heart of others,
Also comes from there, from that secret.

When heart is purified,
That secret covers the world.
At that time, nobody dies.
Because of the rotation of the land of Absence,
All of them become eternal.

Beg Shems of Tebriz. Say,
"Kindly look at us once
From the garden of Absence."

137.

Verse 3406

Don't look for salvation
Except at the burning deep inside,
Because Heart is not enlightened
From outside fire.

When a patient's suffering and pain increase,
The Sultan of Absence comes from
The secret door inside of the heart
And kindly asks, "How are you?"

Look for the scent of that Musk Gazelle,
The hair of that Beauty, in trouble and poverty.
There is no such thing in enjoyment.

An Angel won't claim the Soul
Until man dies.
Who would fall in love with a murderer?
The one who is content with death.

His Love has told you,
"Either We go, or you go."
Advance. It doesn't matter if you
Are on the move or standing still.

When your heart is wounded,
Heart will know the secret of Soul
And understand.
Then, no shame, no blame,
No rebellion stays in Self.

If grief makes you suffer,
Separates you from yourself,
It rains glory on you from the blue sky.

Sit in the middle
Of troubles and sorrows
And think of the Beloved.
O poor lazy one, why are you after a spell?

If God's Shems showed himself,
Tebriz would add Soul to your Soul.
You'd be happy; not miserable like that.

138.

Verse 3415

O sword of time,
Pull out of the sheath of space.
Dive in the sea like a fish.
Swim this endless sea of meanings.

Don't wish to unite.
Union is attributed to the body.
I see such closeness
That it is closer than closeness.

Even man doesn't want several owners.
Why would God want a second one
In His Providence?

Is there a lover who
Would have two Beloveds?
Fall in love in such a way
That love will free you
From all captivities.

Love is the light of my Soul,
My morning wine.
Love is such a hope that
All hope gathers there.

Do you know what Love is?
Love is leaving "Me," "We,"
And all claims of "Being" behind.
Destroying all desire and longing
In the Creator of Beauty.

That smoke, those words, are mine.
My fires are in the heart
Behind that smoke.
My love is increasing every day.

My heart wants you more and more.
My God, don't stop me from that wish.
My God, You see me
Absolving You from all defects.
You increase my fire more and more.

I absolve from defects
The One who sees me.
I absolve from defects
The One who sees and watches.
I absolve from defects
The One who calls me
With His grace, not to try me.

Be silent. The color of my face,
My tears, explain my situation.
The shape I'm in from the Love
Which is greater than pure meaning,
Cannot fit in meaning.

139.

Verse 3425

Player, when you hit
Your plectrum to the strings,
You are encouraging the ones
Who become lazy on this road.

O Love, you came
To this land of Separation
To help the stranded ones.
To lead them to the Beloved.

You give security to the Earth
In spite of the blindness
Of the one who holds-up
The stage on the roads.
You catch the thieves
On the tavern of Heart
And drag them to the gallows.

You see the swindlers.
You blind them with one trick.
When you see a friend
You lead him to the cave.[86]

You put a golden saddle
On the fast horses.
The ones which have a bad saddle,
You make pack animals.

You caress our lovers all the time,
But drag the ones who are dealers
In the market, fond of money,
Here and there; making them cry.

You show the rose garden to the lover
Who suffered from the thorns.
But the one who wanted
To control the rose of joy for himself
You pushed onto the thorns.

You favor the one who plunged into fire
With an open road to the water.
The one who escaped the water,
You threw into the fire.

You give greatness to Moses,
Who walks on the earth modestly.
Face the Pharaoh, who wants greatness,
With shame and disgrace.

You lead Moses to the snake
With the horse which has reversed shoes.[87]
Nobody could question your divine wisdom.

140.

Verse 3435

O One who took our choice,
Our willpower, You are our choice.
You are our willpower.
I am a branch of saffron,
You are our tulip garden.

"You grief has killed me," I said.
"How dare Grief," he answered.
"Didn't it know that you
Are our last friend?"

"I am a garden, a meadow," I said.
"But autumn burnt me.
Bring back the smile to my garden.
You are the ultimate spring."

"You are our harp," he said.
"It is our voice which comes through you."
"In a situation like that,
What is that cry?
You are already in our arms."

I said, "Every imagination hurts my head."
"Cut the neck of the images," he said.
"You are our Zül-fekar.

I put my hand to my head.
"I have a hangover," I said.
"Didn't we give you this hangover?" he asked.
"You are our drunk."

"I swear to God," I said,
"Like a whirling sky, I have no decisions."
"Didn't you decide on us?" he said.

Your lips are like sugar." I said.
He bit his lips.
"Hide this secret," he said.
"Aren't you our own confidant?"

O, the nightingale who sings
In the early morning
Often inquires about us.
You are from our country.

You are the bird which flies in the sky,
Not the one on the ground.
You are from our garden, our meadow.

You have been annihilated from your Being.
You've been wrapped up by the Beloved.
You exist with His existence.
You are either the Glory of God,
Or You are our God.

You were born from mud,
Fell into fire.
Since you are gambling with us,
Take gain and losses as the same.

Duality doesn't fit here.
What is this me and we?
Since you are with our numbers,
Count them both the same.

Be silent! There is a Soul
In every subtle point.
Don't give Soul to everyone.
Didn't you give Soul to us?

141.

Verse 3449

I held his skirt.
"O pearl of kindness and generosity,
Don't leave by saying "Goodnight."
Don't hurt us. Tonight you are for us," I said.

His face, which attracts the heart,
Is flushed, becomes red like fire.
"Enough," he said. "Get your hand off.
What is this hunger?"

I told the messenger of God,
"If you want something, ask it
Of the ones who have beautiful faces."

He answered me, "The beautiful-faced one
Desires whatever he desires after his own wishes.
He has a bad temper because his only worth
Is his coyness, his oppression."

"If this is the case," I said,
"His oppression offers Soul to the Soul.
Just try. Everything you try
Is the spell of a treasure."

He said, "These are just empty words.
Where is this beautiful face?
This shape, this color are all a trap;
Disloyalty and a fake."

If there is no Soul of the Soul
In someone, make sure there is no attraction.
But so many people sacrifice their lives
To shape, it may soon disappear.

I said, "O beautiful face,
You make nothing into something again.
Change our copper to gold.
You are the secret chemical itself."

When the secret chemical comes,
Copper gives itself.
You are a grain, but out of the mill.

He said, "You don't even give thanks.
Don't know the copper.
You have doubt about things.
You show, you talk, you compare."

I started to cry. "Command is yours,"
I said. "Come to my crying.
Help me, O Source of Brightness."

He smiled when he saw my tears.
With that kindness, with that intimacy,
East and West came to life.

O friends, cry.
Shed tears like rain
So the beauties will send you
A beautiful-faced charmer
From the green fields.

142.

Verse 3462

Play the three-stringed instrument.
I reached Union. Don't double talk.
Either play from a Rehavi[88] tune,
Or sing from the tune of salvation.

If you don't have the zir and bem[89]
For the lute notes, don't play them.
We are engulfed in grief.
Find a Neva tune with the reed.
Find and blow the sounds.
Wail from lack of music and melodies.

The remedy of this separation
Is the song from Irak's tune.
You will take the heart away
Without saying one word.
But where, and how far, will you take it away?

O Beauty who all the Sultans know,
Caress our Soul with the tune of Isfahan.
Be intimate with us.

Go to the gathering of our drunk friends
By composing some Zengule tunes.
Finish this matter.
Why this anxiety, this sluggishness?

Restrain our heart,
O one who falls down from non-union.
He is One, but he appears
To us as two.

Play a tune of Rast
If you are a good and faithful friend,
So you will arrive to the tune of Hicaz.

Get into Ussak through
The melodies of Juseyni.
Bring joy to the heart
With the tunes of Buselik and Maye.

The are asking for Dugah,
You sing from Cargah.
You are the candle, the light
Of this place, this country.
O my Beautiful, how nice
That you sing and play.

143.

Verse 3471

O matchless, peerless Creator,
You sometimes make a dog
Superior to a lion.
Other times, You make a black stone
Appear as a water carrier.

So many Sultans. Feridun,[90]
With their bloody swords
And tulip-like faces, eventually
Become beggars, slaves, and shoe cleaners.

That will be the day
The greatest of the Greats
And tyrants who are more fiery than fire
Will turn around the neighborhood of love.
They will fall into poverty and become beggars.

It is for the fire to destroy.
It is for the candle to cry.
It is for us to be faithful and in service.
For the Beloved
Unfaithfulness is expected.

The fire doesn't smile;
It is ashes and smoke.
The candle doesn't cry;
It is a piece of wood or thick stick.

The one who comes to the garden of Earth
And doesn't look for the owner,
Is the donkey out in the thorn pasture.

O donkey, first look for the owner
Of the garden. His kindness, His greatness
May help you to be better than a donkey.

A stranger came from somewhere;
Became the guest of a distinguished person,
Who treated him with respect.

Every day, he served better, fresher fish
To him than the day before.

One night, the stranger told him,
"This is fine, but if you come
To our town, I will treat you much better."

The distinguished man wondered,
"What could be better than
These meals, these clothes?"
He was bewildered.

Those words made the host sick.
They stuck in his throat.
He didn't know what it was
To be entertained in the sky;
To be a guest in the sky.

The fruits of this world
Are like colorful roses;
But Earth's benefaction is nothing
But bread and grabbing the bread.

"O, my God," he said.
"Take me to this stranger's town
So I can untie this knot in my heart."

Several years elapsed
In expectation of this trip.
Even medicine doesn't have effect
Without waiting.

"O One," he said,
"Who creates reason,
You are the One to create
The way out of this trap of troubles."

His praying increased.
In the end, God accepted his praying.
"O one saying 'my God'," he said,
"See the power of God?"

The King wanted to send an emissary
To that town to carry a message.

This man, who bribed openly,
Managed, in his secret way, to have
The king send him on that mission.

The King said, "All right. You sound
Like a nice parrot. Go there
And relate our news to them."

The man did all the preparations
For the journey. Gathered a squadron of soldiers
And had them carry a big, moon-like torch
In front to light the roads.

He started the journey,
Moving from one stage to another,
Flowing like a torrent and
Prostrating toward the side of secret sages.

Like Moses, in order to find
The Hizir who is the enlightener,
He flew with hundreds of wings,
Like a Hoopoe bird.

Like the Archangel Gabriel,
That messenger of the throne
Set forth on a journey
In order to apply His orders.

A bright eye is always on the journey.
O one whose face is like a moon,
You also are the light of this land.
You also are set on the journey.

Every stage of your journey
Is like a different sign of the Zodiac.
There is a door there. There is a cover.
Sorrows are like fire and lightning.
Your joys are like lights.

To make the story short,
The Emissary reached there
Like a piece of straw, attracted
By the Beloved's magnet.

We are like a caravan, constantly moving.
The hand of the One who pulls us is hidden.
Nobody will be able to get away from that hand.

He pulls this one to the left;
The other one, He leads to the right.
He pulls this one to Union;
The other, He pushes to separation.

This side shows all the signs of Union.
In order to make the one who comes, drunk and warm.
The other side shows the forms of separation
With all the tricks and deceits.

That distinguished man was going
Like a ship in a rough sea.
After he arrived, he ran here and there
Saying, "What is my purpose? Where is my wish?"
He was looking for his purpose, his wish.

The One who searches by heart,
Eventually finds what he looks for.
We know You are searching for us.

Suddenly, in one place he smelled something.
His mind flew from his head.
He became drunk, his legs gave up.

He forgot the news the king
Had given to him to carry.
How could he enter the assembly
To give the news?

He stayed there for forty days,
Drunk from that smell.
Those with him were all puzzled.
Wondered what had happened to him.

There was no order left. No authority,
No ritual ablution, no cleanliness,
No words, no sign, no desire for Earth.

The one who wishes one thing so strongly,
Becomes bewildered and says yes to everything.
In confusion, Yes and No are the same.

Where is the tent? Where to ride?
Where is business or occupation?
Where are tricks and deceits?
Where is Dimme Kelile?[91]
Where is the emissary?

The torrent of Love came
And no house, no roof was left.
When the torrent mixes with the sea,
There will be no source, no beginning,
No end or merging.

The man told the stranger,
"My friend, you did what you promised.
You took us from the bottom
And put us at the top of greatness."

This is a lesson. It is not in the Vasit,[92]
Nor in the Muntakaa.[93]
I have never read this lesson.

Your case is better than your means.
Your means more beautiful than your case.
Soul turns his face to you.
You are the Kible for praying.

These are the beginnings.
Tell the end of the story.
I won't tell. You ask for the end
From the One who gives you
The seeing eyes, the hearing ears.

My God, I do wrong to myself.
You tear the curtain of the senses.
If copper acted like copper,
What would happen?
You are the Alchemist.

The head of the table where the big ones sit
Is the place where troubles are.
I made an oath to God.
We get higher only with contrition.

O my people, my great men,
From those who keep their promises,
Those who are in the habit of righteousness,
Loyalty has never been deprived.

144.

Verse 3518
(Terci-i Bend)

Our master, our leader,
As long as you are around
Our fortune smiles. Our luck is good.
O my Beautiful, your coquetries,
Your gracefulness remain.
You are the Soul of Grace and coquetry.

You cause lips to smile.
Brighten sorrowed eyes.

I made an oath to myself. I said,
"I won't laugh as long as I live."
But when you uncovered your face
And appeared to me, I broke my oath.

Whichever deathbody you want to try,
If you go next to his grave,
He tears his coffin, rises up
And grabs the glass.

You pass by my grave when I die,
And watch how I rise up.
Watch the real resurrection.

How could a person die
When You are the cupbearer?
The place You water is always green;
Never fades, burns, nor decays.

Be our companion.
We pass, even though there are
Hundreds of deserts in front of us,
Because You are our hands and feet.

I asked the moon and stars,
"How long will you go on making
Your heads like feet?
Is that because the road is too far,
Or because of confusion?

"O moon," I said, "Your effort is great.
You are the top height. You are great.
But even then, time after time,
You become thin, decrease in size.
At other times, you mature, become a full moon.
You disappear during the day, like a bat.
At night, you raise your flag."

One thing grows and matures,
On thing declines.
One dies, disappears,
The other ailment finds the remedy.

Be a student to my moon-faced one
And walk under his flag.
Walk, and with the help of God,
Be saved from changing
From one condition to the other.

He told me, "If you have doubt,
I'll get rid of it.
I'll clean up all your problems.
Enter another Terci
So I can tell all about me.

O, the moment the bird
Of Soul flies away,
When the Beautiful One goes to His temple,
Souls will return at the time
Coffins and clothes are torn.

O One who says, "What is Soul?"
What is the world?
O, the Soul just comes to the lip.
This is the time of Union.
This is the time of which
You have been asking.

O heart, you opened your hand,
Grabbed a few things from this one and that one.
Nothing but struggle is left to you now.

Sometimes you earned gold and silver.
Sometimes you took the silver-bodied
Beauty in your arms.
At the time of death
Those were dreamy memories for you.

O one who hurt everything
From bird to fish with his wildness,
Now you have to suffer through
All they suffered and have gone through.

How lucky for such a person
That he, who acquired the power to do
The impossible from God, learned
To run like a lion before death.

He learned to close his ears
To the words of flirts and Beauties.
Gave up the things which would
Eventually leave man and disappear.

You were born from the soil.
You are drunk from the garden.
Filled from the earth.
If you want to eat the food of heart,
Wash your mouth. Its milk
Won't stay on your lips.

The teeth of Heart won't grow
When you are sucking milk.
The teeth of Heart grow
To make you able to eat the food of Soul.

Your fondness is to eat roasted meat,
To drink wine, to increase your milk sucking.

O one who pursues his desires;
O one who closes both ears,
Take the cotton from your ears
And listen to this.

Even if you don't remove the cotton,
Don't add more of it.
Another Terci comes, come to your senses.

Night time, coming untimely, you are ours.
You are an untimely risen sweetheart.
It is night now, come home. Where are you?

You don't have food in the cage.
Have no desire for anybody but us.
You don't have anybody.
You are alone. Come, leave this duality.

Give your Soul to love.
Show your loyalty to us.
Leave yourself. Come to us.
That's better for you.

Give up the dry and wet.
Come quickly to the house.
Instead of being more loyal than others,
Why are you so unfaithful?

Your kindness is different than others'.
Nobody appreciates you.
Love attracts you toward us
Because you deserve us.

If sleep has slipped away
From the eyes because of the sparks of love,
Just answer our questions
O Soul, who earned everybody's satisfaction.

If that Sultan named Shems of Tebriz
Insists and hides,
You give Soul to him
So you can reach eternal life.

145.

Verse 3549

O one who plays the Harp of Meaning,
You have given enough water
To the one whose heart has been thirsty
For you with your beautiful melodies.

Soul is your eternal thirst.
This thirst has gone beyond the limit.
Either you cut this with the sword of separation,
Or offer the cup of grace and kindness.

O adorned, decorated Venus,
Play us those two tunes.
Either the tune of Rehavi
Or the tune of Salvation.

If you play the harp in such a bad way,
You will dissolve and melt
Under the nails of grief.
Play well. Sing nice. Otherwise
You'll be dead without food, without music.

Without hitting the strings with the plectrum,
No instrument has cheer and joy.
No sound, no voice comes from the instrument.
If you are loyal to your friend,
Hit the strings of the instrument
With the plectrum, the plectrum.

If they break your strings,
They put you on their laps.
They will adjust you again.
What's your worry? Why are you so sad?

You are a dear friend.
You are always on a lap
In the assembly of the Sultan.
You are in the world
Beyond the Soul, beyond the place.

Be silent. I am very drunk.
Tie both my hands.
If you come, if I see you a moment,
I'll break the glass.

I am the head of the one
Who is out of work or business.
I keep hurting myself.
I don't appreciate not showing
Respect to the drunk.

I am torn to pieces.
Sometimes I am against any help.
Also, I am like a rock
For resistance and hunger.

I am tough and rebellious.
I have been at the hell of separation
For some time, being burned so much.
Even hell stays away from my burning.

The one who sells perfume
At the assembly of Greatness
Broke his tables when he saw
My exuberance, my bittersweetness.

I have spoken hundreds of words to Shemseddin
At the Assembly of God's Union at Tebriz,
Without sound and alphabet.

146.

Verse 3562

A sound came from the reed of Kingdom.
O Soul, clap your hands.
O Heart, tap the floor. Start dancing.

A jewel, a mine, starts sparkling,
The whole world smiles.
A table is set and prepared.
The sound of invitation is coming.

We have smelled a spring;
Have seen green grass and meadow.
We fell in love with a beautiful face.
That's why we are drunk, yelling "Hey. Hey."

He is the sea; we are clouds.
He is treasure; we are a ruined place.
We are particles in the sunlight.

I am drunk beyond bounds.
Forgive me for whatever I said.
Let me. Let me split the moon in two
With the glory of Mustafa.

147.

Verse 3567

All day we were with You.
Day has passed, with all kinds of happiness.
Alas. Alas, I am afraid
You'll leave me by saying goodnight.

You are saying goodnight.
How will the fire be good?
Your separation is like fire;
Even worse than that.

The Lover couldn't live
Without You at night.
He would die.
But Your beautiful image comes,
Asks about him. That's the only way
The Lover could survive.

You told my ears a few words.
To pair with You, to unite with You.
Don't deny it.
How could I know this secret otherwise?

I have heard Your secret.
I will have the night as my witness.
But night has seen so many guilty ones
He worships secretly.
I wonder if it would be my witness.

Notes

1. Koran LIII, 8.
2. This verse is said as a prayer before eating by the Mevlevis.
3. Futu-i vet: A social organization with Sufi influence (12-13 century and after).
4. Elest: "Am I not your God?" Koran VII, 172-173.
5. Ashab-i Kehf: Seven friends and a dog took refuge in a cave so they wouldn't have to worship idols. God put them to sleep for three hundred years. When they woke up, they thought they had slept for only half a day, Koran, XVIII, 9-26.
6. Koran XVII-III.
7. Koran XLVII, 19.
8. A city in central Asia– Turkestan. Famous for beautiful women.
9. Kible: Direction to Mecca for prayers.
10. Negro symbolizes darkness, versus people of Rum, who symbolize brightness, day.
11. Literally, "Saying 'ten-ten-ten...'"
12. Fifteenth day of the eighth lunar month. A holy day.
13. Koran XXIV, 26.
14. Kevser: River in Heaven.
15. Sahib Kiran: A sultan who was crowned at the time the sun and Venus were in the same sign of the zodiac.
16. Kayser: Julius Caesar was called Kayser in the East. Denotes the one with the most power.
17. Esir: The layer above the sky, lighter than air, which becomes a conduit for light and heart.
18. Beyazid-i Bistami: d. 874-75.
19. Koran XXIV, 26.
20. Koran II, 7.
21. Two holidays in the Arabic calendar: First day of Sevval and 10th day of Zilhicce.

22. Fatiha: First Sure of Kuran.
23. Ridvan: The angel at the door of heaven.
24. Hizir: legendary person who attained immortality by drinking from the fountain of life.
25. Koran, LIII, 3.
26. Bidat: Events which happened after Prophet Mohammed.
27. Yagma: A Turkish clan.
28. Keykubad: King of Kings, First king of Persia.
29. Rustem: A Persian king who became a legendary hero.
30. Refers to Joseph being sold in a bazaar.
31. Siddiyk: Nickname of First Caliph, Abu Bekr—means "proven."
32. Halil: the prophet Abraham.
33. Arabic love story.
34. Mecnun: A character in an Arabic love story.
35. Koran.
36. Abu Lehib: Prophet Mohammed's uncle. A disbeliever.
37. Acem: Everyone who is non-Arab.
38. Alepo: The city where the best glass was made.
39. Basra: A city famous for its dates.
40. Yakiyn: A certainty.
41. Rint: An unconventional, jolly person or Dervish.
42. Eighteen is a lucky number for Mevlevis.
43. Aeter: The clear, upper regions of the sky-ether.
44. Namaz: Ritual praying.
45. Abdest: Ritual Abolution.
46. The Melameti order takes a few hairs from the head, beard, and mustache of the aspirant.
47. Hüma: A bird of legend. If its shadow is cast upon someone, he becomes a Sultan.
48. Tree of Tuba: The legendary tree that covers the universe.

49. Kafdagi: A fabulous mountain inhabited by djinns.
50. Halva: Sweetmeats.
51. Hizir: Legendary person who comes to help in critical moments; a godsend.
52. Hamza: Uncle of the Prophet Mohammed, known for his bravery.
53. Abu-Ali (ibni sina) d. 1037. Famous philosopher.
54. Abu-ala: d. 1057. Famous poet.
55. Zül-fekar: The sword of Ali.
56. Koran, IX, 40.
57. Rebab: Three-string violin.
58. Namaz: Prayer.
59. Hitay: A city in Eastern Turkistan, famous for beautiful women and gazelles that give musk.
60. Mugh: Zarathrustan priest.
61. Irak: A mode in music.
62. Sheriat: Religious law.
63. Imam: Religious Ledaer.
64. Karun: Legendary rich.
65. Hicaz: Mode of Near-Eastern music.
66. Nefs-i Mutmainne: Pious, saintly self: Koran LXXXIX, 27.
67. Old belief.
68. Sema: Dance ritual of whirling dervishes.
69. Nazar: Glance of the guide.
70. Zebur: (Mezàmir): Name of the Prophet David's book.
71. Salâh of Religion: Righteousness of religion, referring to Salâhaddin.
72. Mecnun and Leyla: Arabic love story.
73. Hodja: Teacher or guide
74. Faruk: Nickname of Second Caliph, Ömer.

75. Zul-fekaar: Caliph Ali's famous sword.
76. Beyazid: (died 874-75).
77. Amid: Vizir in Selchuck's famous literature. Generosity (d. 1063).
78. Imad: Founder of Al-i Buvah government in Iran (d. 949).
79. Badya: A large wooden or earthen bowl.
80. Zir: Tunes in near-Easter music.
81. Trust: According to sufis, Names of God.
82. Merguzle and Rey'li, and Magribli and Tuslu are allusions to opposites.
83. Koran, VII, 143.
84. Koran, XV, 29 - XXXVIII, 72.
85. According to Sufis, man comes first. The universe is his manifestation.
86. Koran, IX, 40.
87. To lose trackers, the shoes on the horses would be put on backwards.
88. Rehavi is a mode of near-Eastern music. In this poem, the following modes of music are mentioned: Nevâ, Irak, Isfahan, Zengule, Rast, Hicaz, Ussak, Juseyni, Buselik, Mâye, Dugah, and Cargah.
89. Zir and bem: Top or bottom strings.
90. Feridun is an idol in Indi-Persian mythology.
91. Dimme Kelile is the Indian book of manners, written by Baydaba.
92. Vasit: Book by Ebu Hamid Muhammed el Gazali (d. 1111-12).
93. Muntakaa: Abu-i Fadi Muhammed al Hakim (d. 945-46).

Notes From Eflaki

In the *Bahr-i Recez*, according to Eflaki (Yazici T., 1953-57, Volume I and Volume II. A publication of the Ministry of Education of the Republic of Turkey.):

Gazel 20 was read at the wedding of Sultan Veled, son of Mevlana (V. II, p. 165).

Gazel 69 was recited during a Sema. Mevlana dropped a handful of dirt into the Kemal-i Kavval's tambourine (V. II, p. 94).

Gazel 79 was recited after staying seven days at Zirva Hamam (bath house) while leaving Hamam because of his son's (Sultan Veled) pleading (V. II, p. 92).

Gazel 150 was recited for the birth of his grandson, Ulu Arif Celebi (V. II, p. 284).

Gazel 162 was for Katib-i Esrar Fahreddin Sivasi, when he had a mental disorder while acting as one of the secret secretaries (V. I, p. 259).

In the *Bahr-i Muzari*,

Gazel 30 was recited when Shemseddin-i Mardini entered Medrese, where Mevlana was teaching (v. I, p. 162).

Gazel 130, tenth verse, was recited during Mevlana's last illness (V. II, p. 12).

Gazel 133 was Mevlana's last gazel, recited on his last night (V. II, p. 13-14).